RETIRING RIGHT

Retiring Right

SMART STEPS FOR EXITING
CORPORATE AMERICA

Jake Falcon

HOUNDSTOOTH
PRESS

RETIRING RIGHT
Smart Steps for Exiting Corporate America

FIRST EDITION

ISBN   978-1-5445-4524-0 *Hardcover*
        978-1-5445-4523-3 *Paperback*
        978-1-5445-4522-6 *Ebook*

Contents

Introduction

You're a corporate associate who has devoted your entire professional life to contributing toward the company's success and longevity. You've progressed through the ranks with focus, determination, and lots of hard work. You've prioritized your employees, team, family, and company's financial success. You've sacrificed your personal interests and free time to serve others, serve your business, and deliver for clients.

Now, you're nearing retirement and facing the end of all you've known for the last twenty, thirty, maybe even forty years. You wonder, "What's next?" "What will the next chapter of my life look like?"

For many corporate associates, the idea of retiring is downright terrifying. Not only are you facing financial stressors ("Will I have enough to last a lifetime?" "What's the most tax-efficient way to establish a monthly income stream?" [And no, I don't mean buying an annuity!] "What about my stock options?"), you're facing emotional ones as well ("Who will I be without my job?" "How will I stay busy and engaged?" "How will my company move forward without me?").

It's natural to worry as you near retirement. It's difficult to walk away from something you've dedicated your life to. But I'm here to tell you...It can and will be okay.

I've enjoyed helping hundreds of corporate associates create a plan and retire with confidence. It's not always easy, and you'll undoubtedly face some challenges along the way, but with a bit of planning and the right guidance, you can achieve a financially successful and emotionally fulfilling retirement.

I hope this book helps you in that pursuit.

THE UNIQUE RETIREMENT CHALLENGES FACED BY CORPORATE ASSOCIATES

The process of retiring is different for everyone. Each person has their own vision for retirement. We all face unique challenges. Our individual fears and anxieties about this momentous life event vary.

While most long-time corporate associates have the advantage of higher-than-normal salaries, stock options, and employer-sponsored retirement plans, they often face a variety of challenges as they prepare to retire. Through my experience working with hundreds of corporate associates, I have found that these challenges commonly fall into two main categories.

1. The emotional/psychological challenges of retirement
2. The financial decisions required to retire

It may surprise you to see "emotional/psychological" challenges in a book written by a wealth advisor, and believe me, I'm no psychologist. However, I've learned throughout the years that the corporate executives who most successfully retire (and live there happily) are those who have addressed the emotional component of this major life change. We'll address this thoroughly in Chapter One, but for now, just be aware that there's a significant psychological element to the retirement process that, if not meticulously planned for and addressed, can leave you feeling unsettled, unhappy, and unfulfilled.

Besides the emotional challenges of retirement, corporate associates also face a wide range of financial challenges. Not only do you need to secure monthly income that lasts for the rest of your life, you need to navigate estate planning, tax planning, healthcare expenses, investment management, life and long-term care insurance, and more.

Whew! Just the idea of tackling all of this can make you want to keep working for a few more years.

But remember, countless corporate associates have effectively navigated the financial and emotional challenges of retirement. You can too. This book walks you through all the basics to help you prepare for your next chapter.

THE IMPORTANCE OF HAVING A PLAN IN PLACE

Planning for a successful retirement is about more than having the right investment allocation and monthly income (although those are important components). Rather, all aspects of your financial life should work together to help achieve your goals. It's vital to have a comprehensive financial plan in place to guide your actions and inform your decision-making. Your plan should incorporate the following strategies.

- Retirement account planning
- Social Security planning
- Tax planning
- Healthcare planning

- Large purchase planning
- Risk management/insurance planning
- Estate/legacy planning
- Investment management

I'll visit each of these strategies later in this book. For now, I just want to stress the importance of having a single, comprehensive plan in place and updating it regularly. It's not effective to take a "set-it-and-forget-it" approach. Your plan should be a dynamic tool that is constantly updated as your life and financial situation change. At a minimum, update your plan once a year and whenever major life events occur.

Once your custom, comprehensive plan is in place, you'll have the information you need to answer the following questions and more.

- When can I retire?
- What will my monthly income be in retirement?
- How much can I afford to spend each month?
- Do I have enough to buy a second home, a boat, or another large purchase? Should I pay cash or finance the purchase?
- Should I pay off my mortgage?
- How do I pay less in taxes?
- When should I collect Social Security?
- Should I choose a lump sum or annuity pension distribution?
- Should I accept my company's buyout offer?
- Should I contribute or convert to a Roth IRA?
- Do I need life and/or long-term care insurance?
- How do I navigate my stock options and concentrated stock positions?
- What's the best way to leave a financial legacy for my loved ones?

- How should I invest my money leading up to and during retirement?

I call bluff on anyone who claims they can answer these questions without consulting a detailed financial plan. It's just not possible in my opinion. To provide informed, accurate advice, your wealth advisor must have the necessary information. The best way to gather that information is by conducting a thorough analysis of your current financial situation, long-term goals, future outlook, and any challenges that may stand in your way, and using that information to create a custom financial plan.

Once your financial plan is in place, your wealth advisor should be able to use planning software to run projections based on various scenarios, manipulating the inputs along the way to give you an idea of how your actions today may affect your future. I believe this detailed, data-driven approach results in the most accurate prediction of your potential success in retirement.

WHY TAKE ADVICE FROM ME?

You may wonder, "What does this guy know about retirement planning?" and, "Why should I listen to him?" I get it. Numerous wealth advisors exist, each boasting expertise in many different areas.

My main qualifier isn't that I work for the biggest firm or bring in the highest commissions. While I charge feeds based on a client's assets under management, I aim to mitigate conflicts of interest. My main qualifier is that I am passionate about helping people transition to retirement. Since I started working in financial services, it's all I've ever wanted to do, and I built my advisory firm exclusively so I could focus on retirement planning without all the typical distractions and disparate responsibilities that come with working at many larger firms.

I also hold the Chartered Retirement Planning Counselor™ (CRPC®) designation, which is awarded by the College for Financial Planning. This designation includes a comprehensive assessment of an advisor's ability to assess an individual's financial needs before and after retirement, including sources of retirement income, personal savings, income taxes, estate planning, and much more.

I've been practicing as a wealth advisor since 2006. In 2016, my business partner, Cory Bittner, CRPC®, and I founded Falcon Wealth Advisors with the sole purpose of helping people succeed and retire with confidence. Since we opened our doors, our team has grown to include experienced professionals dedicated to supporting our clients in areas such as financial, tax, and retirement planning, along with investment management and more. All our employees share a common goal—to help clients achieve a successful retirement.

I've also been interviewed by Bloomberg, Yahoo Finance, and CNN Business, to name a few.

To me, it comes down to this: how many times will you plan for retirement? If you do it right, the answer is once. How many times have I planned for retirement? I've met with hundreds of people and had thousands of meetings. I've encountered nearly every challenge, roadblock, and setback imaginable. And, with the help of my amazing team, I've skillfully helped countless clients overcome those challenges and arrive at the retirement of their dreams.

Ultimately, you have only one chance to retire. Make sure you put in the effort to retire right.

MY BACKGROUND AND EXPERIENCE

As I work with new clients, my first goal is always to get to know them—their likes and dislikes, what makes them tick, what's most important to them, their families, and loved ones. Asking basic questions about someone's life and priorities is the first step toward building a trusted relationship. I thought it might be helpful to share a bit about myself.

How I Got My Start...

I was born in Kansas City but mainly raised in Nebraska and Texas. During my formative years, both of my parents worked at a Phillips 66 refinery near Amarillo, Texas. I started golfing at a young age and entered school at the University of Texas, San Antonio, with a goal of becoming a golf pro. However, that goal changed during college when I got my first job working at a country club. That job made me realize that, for me, golf was a better hobby than profession.

Soon after that experience, finance emerged as one of my favorite courses in college. I absolutely loved how I could apply the concepts I was learning to real-world scenarios and have a direct impact on outcomes. So, I decided to shift gears and focus on becoming a wealth advisor. In 2006, a couple of years after I graduated, I moved back to Kansas City to begin my career in financial services.

After becoming licensed, I went on to earn my CRPC® designation to further my knowledge of retirement planning. I also completed the Investment Strategies and Portfolio Management program at the University of Pennsylvania's Wharton School of Business.

Making a living as an advisor was tough at first...I mean, really tough. I was offered a job at a prominent firm, but my main way of getting clients was literally going door to door in North Kansas City, asking people if they had any money they needed help investing. What a different time that was!

Surprisingly, that approach worked. Clients signed on with me and I started managing assets on their behalf. The problem was, while my money management approach was adding assets to their portfolios, I didn't feel like I was adding value to their lives.

I will always be grateful to that first firm for taking a chance on a new advisor and for helping me discover my place in the industry; however, I knew pretty quickly I needed to find a better fit.

My Next Endeavor...

My desired approach was much better suited to the next firm I joined. Door knocking ceased, and a mentor embraced me, commencing my education on financial planning and active investment management. *This* was what I wanted to do.

I discovered my love of retirement planning at this firm. My parents were nearing retirement age, and I spent a lot of time with soon-to-be retirees on the golf course. (Golf was absolutely, and will always remain, one of my favorite hobbies.) I found it fascinating to learn about the challenges faced by those nearing retirement, and I wanted to help my friends and family members retire well.

I began discovering that, while retirement is just one of many financial events many people experience in their lifetimes, everything else they do throughout their financial lives eventually leads them to that point. The decisions they make throughout their careers and personal lives impact whether they can retire when they want and, perhaps more importantly, *how* they want.

To me, there's something so compelling about helping clients successfully retire. Working with clients throughout their lifetimes to prepare for that life transition is incredibly rewarding work, and I'm so grateful that my professional path took me in that direction.

I'll never forget a conversation I had early in my career. I asked another advisor what type of financial services he provided and he rolled his eyes before telling me he offered retirement planning services. His dislike for the work was evident, and I sensed he contemplated a career change. I just didn't understand it. How could you *not* love helping clients cross that significant financial finish line?

I *do* love helping clients retire successfully, and that's why I have dedicated my career to retirement planning.

Why I Started My Own Firm...

I worked at my previous firm for ten years and, with the help of my team, built a niche retirement practice. My team and I operated within the larger firm, yet we still had certain firm requirements we needed to adhere to. Under the larger firm, we were acting in the best interests of our clients in some situations and as sales agents or brokers in other situations. Over time, this seemed like more and more of a conflict of interest to me.

As a team, we wanted to exclusively focus on serving the best interests of our clients. My partner, Cory Bittner, CRPC®, and I finally decided our goals for the future of our business differed from the course laid out by our current firm. We were determined to answer only to clients.

It was time to start our own firm.

I will not lie…that was one of the scariest decisions I've ever made. Cory and I took out a huge loan to start the firm. We managed to convince multiple highly skilled, experienced team members to join us. We secured a small office rental and prayed our clients would stick with us. To our relief, most of them did. Falcon Wealth Advisors was up and running!

Where We Are Now...

Today, we're a team of nearly twenty professionals managing close to a billion dollars on behalf of our clients who live in thirty states and counting. We serve as fiduciaries, putting our clients' best interests first. Every person in this firm is passionate about retirement planning.

We purposefully limit our firm's growth, taking on only the clients for whom we can provide exceptional value and service. Because we focus on providing exceptional service to all clients, we end a relationship if it's not a fit. We want to work with people who share our values and are open to implementing solutions to their challenges.

As we've grown, we have discovered that our approach, process, and experience make us suited to provide retirement planning services to a niche market of corporate associates who work or have worked at publicly traded companies. We've thoroughly dug into this specialty niche, learning all we can about how to maximize company benefits and income streams, while also helping clients navigate the emotional challenges of retiring.

We are passionate about helping corporate associates retire successfully.

Outside the Office...

When I'm not in the office, I'm likely spending time with my beautiful wife, Rachel, and our beloved goldendoodle, Einstein. Or I'm out on the golf course, forever trying to improve my game.

Let's shift the focus away from me. It's time to help *you* plan for retirement. Let's get started!

CHAPTER ONE

Finding Your Purpose

The Emotional Side of Retirement

WHY RETIREMENT ISN'T ALL SUNSHINE AND RAINBOWS

Congratulations! You've successfully reached the end of a long and successful career in corporate America! You're ready for retirement, a time of life you've been waiting for, planning for, and anxiously anticipating. It's time to remove all the stress and enjoy life. Hello, golf course! Hello, world travels! Hello, freedom to do what you want, when you want!

But, wait... Why is the house so quiet? Where are the friends you thought you'd have by your side after you left the workforce? Why does your spouse seem irritated by your lack of a daily routine?

It surprises many new retirees to discover that retirement isn't all sunshine and rainbows. In fact, it can be lonely, isolating, and downright depressing. This is undeniably true for former corporate associates who, by nature, tend to be overachieving, extremely motivated individuals.

If you weren't happy before you retired, it's unlikely you will be happy in retirement. Why is that? From my experience working with clients, I've noticed that many times the people who are most unhappy in their careers build up retirement as a finish line to all their unhappiness. They tell themselves, "If I can just make it to retirement, all my problems will go away and I'll finally be able to enjoy life."

These are the people who are most disappointed to discover that retirement is not all sunshine and rainbows. In fact, it takes a lot of effort to find happiness in retirement. As much as you may be ready to put the "work" word behind you, the truth is you need to *work* to find happiness at any phase in life, even in retirement.

Retirement doesn't provide a 180-degree turn from the stress of life. In fact, it often amplifies stress. Here's an example.

Les and Rita have been married for forty years. They have three grown children and two grandchildren, with another on the way. Les is a corporate executive who averages fifty to sixty hours of work a week. Rita spent the early years of their marriage raising children. Once the kids moved out, she began working part time as a bookkeeper for her friend's business. Twice a week, she serves lunch at the local soup kitchen, and she helps on a committee that coordinates an annual benefit for a women's shelter. Rita goes on regular walks with friends and never misses her Wednesday morning yoga class. On Fridays, she watches her grandbabies to relieve their daughter and son-in-law of some daycare expenses.

Les and Rita were both looking forward to Les's upcoming retirement. A week after his last day, they leave for a three-week trip to Europe. It's the vacation of their dreams. Life is good and the couple returns home happy, rested, and connected.

Rita soon resumes her routine of bookkeeping, volunteering, exercising, and caring for the grandkids. Les isn't sure what to do with himself. He attempts to schedule some rounds of golf but struggles to find a daytime group. He works on some home improvement projects but isn't happy with the results, and he gets irritated with Rita because she's never around.

Rita gets irritated too. She doesn't understand why Les sulks around the house so much. She attempts to have coffee with him every morning and dinner with him at night, but he seems restless and unhappy with his circumstances.

The couple soon becomes stressed. Tension fills the house. Neither is happy. They both agree, "This is not how retirement is supposed to be."

While Les and Rita are a fictional, made-up couple, their struggle is real and very common. Retirement isn't a finish line; it's a new chapter. To find happiness, you must be deliberate about how you write it. It takes time, focus, determination, and cooperation. It requires constant revision and the ability to alter the plot line.

The good news is, you're the author and have complete control. With a bit of time, effort, and focus, you can write a happy ending to your corporate career. I hope to help you get started.

FINDING PURPOSE AND FULFILLMENT OUTSIDE OF WORK
THE 10:00 A.M. ON A TUESDAY TEST

What's the difference between Les and Rita in the previous example? Neither is working full time, yet Rita has found purpose and fulfillment. Les was still searching.

What do Les and Rita have in common? Neither will be happy until both find purpose and fulfillment.

The challenge is knowing if you'll find fulfillment after retiring.

One way to assess your potential happiness in retirement is by asking yourself the 10:00 a.m. on a Tuesday question: "Once I retire, what will I be doing at 10:00 a.m. on any given Tuesday?"

If you can't answer that question, you may need to put some more thought into how you will find purpose and fulfillment outside of work. The key to finding fulfillment is to retire *to* something, not just away from work. You don't have to be constantly meeting deadlines and producing. You just have to have a reason to get out of bed every morning. Until you have that reason, you're probably not ready to retire.

TIME BLOCKING

One way to find your purpose in retirement is by time blocking. As a former (or soon-to-be former) corporate employee, you're no stranger to managing a daily calendar. Use the same strategy in retirement—not only for important events, but for anything you'd like to accomplish daily.

- Do you want to watch *The Price is Right* every day at 10:00 a.m.? Put it on your calendar.
- Are you hoping to exercise three times a week? Put it on your calendar.
- At 6:00 p.m., will you have wine with your spouse? Put it on your calendar.

It may seem silly to time block every minor event, but the simple act of putting things on your calendar can add much-needed structure to your day. Perhaps it can keep you from wasting time on things that don't provide fulfillment.

If you open your calendar for the week and realize it's empty, you know you need to attempt to add to it. Be deliberate. What do you want to accomplish this week? It's possible you haven't caught up with a friend in a while. Perhaps your grandson has a soccer game you'd like to watch. Maybe there's a new restaurant you've been meaning to try, or you might want to see who will win the "Showcase Showdown." Whatever it is, mark it on your calendar and stick to the schedule you've created for yourself.

ASK YOURSELF QUESTIONS (AND RESPOND HONESTLY!)

Finding happiness in retirement requires a lot of soul searching. I know, I know…sounds cheesy, right? Try not to roll your eyes; it's true! You need to look inside and be honest with yourself about what brings happiness and fulfillment to your life. Then, focus on what truly makes *you* happy while leaving behind the rest. (Tip: It's sometimes the "leaving behind" that's the hardest part.)

Start by asking yourself the following questions. Seriously think about your answers. Ponder your responses for a few days and consider how different responses would make you feel.

Will Not Working Really Make Me Happy?

If work makes you unhappy, will you be happy if you don't work? Your knee-jerk response may be, "Yes!" but think about it. What is it about work that makes you unhappy? Will those things still be present in your life once you retire?

If you're used to being in a constant state of unhappiness, how will you break free from that? Retirement on its own isn't always enough to break the cycle of unhappiness.

Before you retire, take time to evaluate what's truly important to you, what matters most, and what you want to accomplish in the next chapter of life. Then take steps to align your life around your priorities and structure activities that bring you joy.

Do I Have Friends Outside of Work?

Many retirees struggle with loneliness and isolation, particularly those who formerly held high-stress, high-pressure jobs. Developing and fostering friendships takes time and effort, two commodities that run short for corporate associates at the peak of their careers.

And it's not just your career that impedes friendships. Remember when your kids were young, and you had an entire community of soccer moms and dads at your fingertips? Those relationships often dissipate as the kids grow older and leave the nest. It becomes more difficult to find friends with whom you share common interests.

How are your former coworkers doing? Many retirees find they have less in common with their professional acquaintances once they exit the workforce. Plus, if your former colleagues are still working, they probably aren't available to get together as often as you'd like.

Now's the time to develop new friendships. Where can you meet other retirees? Is it on the golf course or at the gym? Have you considered volunteering for a local charity?

Start by participating in things you enjoy. That way, you can meet people who share common interests. Who knows where you may find a new friend?

Will My Spouse and I Get Along?

This is big. The divorce rate among couples age fifty and older has doubled in the last twenty years.[1] The occurrence is so common, it has been coined the "gray divorce." Sadly, some couples discover there's little left between them after the busy years of building careers, raising kids, and managing a household have passed.

Sometimes, the love is still there, but after thirty to forty years of having your own daily routines, you may feel you're stuck in a telephone booth together when you're both home all day.

Use the years leading up to retirement as an opportunity to rekindle your relationship with your spouse. Get used to it being just the two of you again. Rediscover what you enjoy doing together. Establish a shared retirement vision.

- What are your big goals? Do you want to purchase a second home, or travel the world? Would moving closer to family make you happy?
- What are your small goals? Would you like to play nine holes twice a week or take daily walks to the local coffee shop? How about a shared reading list with regular book discussions?

Remember that it's okay to have different retirement goals. You don't have to spend every waking hour together. In fact, it's inadvisable to do so. Pursue your hobbies and interests. Just make sure you agree on the big stuff and attempt to connect in small ways. This will help keep your relationship strong over the next thirty years.

---

1 "Divorce Statistics: Over 115 Studies, Facts, and Rates for 2024," Wilkinsen & Finkbeiner, accessed January 11, 2024, https://www.wf-lawyers.com/divorce-statistics-and-facts.

What do you love about life? What is your purpose? How do you want to spend your time? What makes you want to jump out of bed in the morning and go out into the world? It's almost certainly been a while since you've asked yourself these questions.

Now that you have no shareholders, board members, bosses, coworkers, or employees to answer to, how will you *choose* to spend your life? What have you waited your whole life to do?

The possibilities are endless. You have complete control. Now's the time to live life to the fullest. What a fantastic opportunity!

ESTABLISHING AN ENCORE CAREER

If the idea of continuing to work after you retire sets your teeth on edge, don't worry. I'm not talking about the same level of stress and pressure you faced in your corporate job. Rather, I'm suggesting you give some thought to whether an encore career may bring purpose and fulfillment to your retirement.

Whether you retired by choice, or were forced to retire unexpectedly, those who have had enough of corporate America but aren't quite ready to spend their days on a golf course can consider an encore career as a great option.

For example, one of my clients retired from a successful corporate career and applied for a job as a hostess at a local restaurant. When she presented her resume, the hiring manager looked at her like she was crazy to want the same job many high schoolers worked. She was told, "You're overqualified for this position." However, this didn't matter to her. Her goal was to find a flexible, low-stress position that allowed her to be social, stay engaged with others, and provide an experience for people in her community. The hostess position checked all the boxes. She has worked there for a while now and continues to find fulfillment in the work. Clearly, the job suits her lifestyle.

ENCORE CAREER OPTIONS

You might wonder, "What are my options for an encore career?" Here are just a few considerations based on what some of our other clients have done.

Stay with Your Current Company

If you enjoy your current company, consider taking a few steps back rather than retiring fully.

For example, if you're a vice president at a technology company, maybe you can mentor those next in line for leadership roles. This allows you to share your knowledge and expertise, remain engaged, and continue helping the business.

Or, if you were formerly in an executive-level position, maybe you can take on a board position at your company. Your insight will likely add value.

Uncover Something Entirely New

Maybe there's another career path you always wondered about. Now's the time to explore it! Today's world is full of opportunities, and your experience as a business leader will likely open many doors. It's not always about having relevant industry experience, it's about your personality and people skills.

Your personal and professional networks can also play a key role in helping you find a new position. Ask around to find out if anyone you know is aware of any interesting opportunities.

Don't be afraid to try something new!

Volunteer

If your encore career is more about providing fulfillment than a salary, consider volunteering for an organization that's important to you.

Volunteering offers a multitude of choices. Perhaps you want to exclusively work with a specific at-risk population. Or maybe you want to take a leadership role and put your business acumen to work at a higher level. Maybe fundraising, event planning, or grassroots activities are more your speed.

Volunteering is a rewarding way to both give back and find your purpose in retirement.

Travel

That's right, I'll say it. Traveling can be a successful encore career. I have several clients who travel nearly full time. They are finding purpose in meeting new people, seeing new sights, trying new foods, and having new experiences.

Some retirees focus their travel on specific hobbies, such as visiting every Major League Baseball stadium, seeing every national park, or exploring all state capitals. Others have a goal of visiting every continent. Some just want to travel between loved ones' homes across the country.

Whatever your travel goals may be, get started sooner than later. Embrace life's adventures while you're still active during your "go-go" years before you slow down to your "no-go" years.

WHY IS MONEY IMPORTANT TO YOU?

This is an important question to ask yourself, as the answer can help you align your finances with your priorities. For example, if one of your goals is to leave a financial legacy for your loved ones, your financial plan, investment allocation, and retirement withdrawal strategy will differ from someone whose main goal is to travel constantly and have as many experiences as possible. Both goals may be right for the individual; they just require a different approach.

At Falcon Wealth Advisors, we are always asking our clients, "Why is money important to you?" Over the years, I've found it interesting that most of our clients' responses fall somewhere on Maslow's hierarchy of needs pyramid. Precisely where on that pyramid each of their responses falls can provide us insight into how comfortable they are with their current lifestyle and level of retirement savings. It can also help us assess whether they are on track to achieve their vision for retirement and make any necessary adjustments to their financial plan based on their goals.

If you, like many college students, took Psych 101 your freshman year, you may recall that American psychologist Abraham Maslow proposed his pyramid of human needs in a 1943 paper entitled, "A Theory of Human Motivation."

Maslow's hierarchy of needs illustrates how humans deeply partake in behavioral motivation. According to his theory, one must satisfy the lower levels of the pyramid before moving up to the next level.

When talking with clients, I often find that they distribute their money motivations across different levels of the pyramid, which I believe is mainly due to how comfortable various clients are with their level of retirement savings.

For example, if you're worried about how you're going to afford buying food and putting a roof over your head in retirement, you will need to work to fulfill those needs before you set your sights on traveling around the world.

Following are examples of how our clients have responded to the question, "Why is money important to you?" and where those responses fit at different levels of the pyramid.

PHYSIOLOGICAL NEEDS

Responses that fall into this category include shelter, food, clothes, and paying bills, such as water and electricity, etc. Some people focus on money to provide for their fundamental needs.

I always find this fascinating, as most of our clients are high-net-worth individuals who can easily cover basic living expenses. Perhaps they respond this way because they're happy to live a simple life and pay for just the necessities. Or, maybe when they were younger, their parents struggled to put food on the table and keep a roof over their heads, and their response is a manifestation of a fear they have always lived with.

Whatever the reason, for some people, money is simply a way to pay for the basic needs of everyday life.

SAFETY NEEDS

For some people, money is important because it provides safety and security and allows them to live debt free, provide for loved ones, and maintain a certain lifestyle. One client often refers to a "ticket to ride," meaning that money is important because it allows him to buy the ticket he needs to enjoy the ride of life.

People whose responses consistently fall into this category want to maintain their current lifestyle throughout retirement.

LOVE AND BELONGING

Moving up the pyramid, many people's responses fall under the love and belonging category. These include priorities such as having experiences and memories with family members, helping kids and grandkids, being together, volunteering, helping others, and having a plan in place to support a spouse should something unexpected happen.

My observation is that many corporate associates who work long hours dream of spending more quality time with their loved ones. They don't worry as much about basic needs or safety and security; instead, they want more time to make memories with the people who matter most to them.

ESTEEM

Some people say money is important to them because it provides freedom, independence, and the ability to travel. Others say money allows them to retire early, stay retired, and that it makes work optional. While money itself can't make you happy, it can make life less stressful.

SELF-ACTUALIZATION

The highest level on the pyramid is self-actualization, which Maslow describes as the realization of one's full potential, or the desire to accomplish everything one can and become the best one can be.

For our purpose, responses that fall into this category include providing a legacy for loved ones, not being a burden to family members, having lifestyle options, maximizing time, constantly improving oneself, and exploring other cultures.

Determining the purpose of your money (i.e., why money is important to you) can help you identify your purpose as well. A successful way to find happiness in retirement is by aligning how you save and spend with your values and purpose so you can live life on your terms.

Take some time to consider why money is important to you. Discuss it with your spouse. Write out your responses. Work with a qualified wealth advisor who can help ensure your financial plan, portfolio, budget, income, cash flow, and goals are aligned with your priorities and vision for the future.

In summary, the simple act of retiring is usually not fulfilling in itself. It takes focus, determination, and yes, plenty of the "work" word to find happiness after leaving a career behind. Fortunately, with the right combination of reflection, effort, and planning, you can be fully prepared, both emotionally and psychologically, for this exciting next chapter of life.

CHAPTER TWO

Financial Planning

The Blocking and Tackling of Retirement

Once you've determined you are fully prepared to retire both emotionally and psychologically, the question becomes, "How do I make it happen?" This is where the real fun begins! (For me, someone who is somewhat obsessed with retirement planning.)

Hopefully, you've been working with a wealth advisor all along and have a detailed financial plan in place. If not, it's time to establish one. There's one important point to make for retiring with confidence: if you don't have a financial plan in place, it probably won't happen. This applies to everyone, regardless of an individual's net worth. Without a solid financial plan, there are numerous potential pitfalls. A financial plan helps protect you from unexpected circumstances that have the potential to rapidly derail your retirement. For more information on having a financial plan in place, refer to Chapter One.

You may wonder, "What, exactly, should my financial plan include?" Great question! In this chapter, I cover the most important financial elements that contribute to a successful retirement.

Note that your specific financial situation may require additional strategies, including college planning for children or grandchildren, debt management, business transition strategies, etc. Your wealth advisor should address those issues. For this book, however, we'll focus on the financial issues that have the most impact on a typical corporate associate's ability to retire right.

THE IMPORTANCE OF SUCCESSFULLY TRANSITIONING FROM SAVING TO SPENDING

You've spent your entire career saving and planning for the day you can finally leave the workforce and live life on your own terms. It's great that you have significant retirement savings, but here's the challenge: how do you turn that savings into a monthly income to last for the rest of your life?

In theory, it sounds simple to shift from saving to spending. In reality, however, this transition can be extremely difficult. How can you be confident the spending decisions you make today won't severely impact you down the road?

This is the place when we often make mistakes. It's important to optimize your retirement savings to achieve your specific retirement goals. It's quite easy to make ill-informed decisions that can significantly harm the long-term viability of your retirement.

In this section, we cover the basic blocking and tackling required to optimize your retirement savings, minimize your taxes, and maximize your ability to live confidently throughout retirement. Let's get started.

OPTIMIZING YOUR RETIREMENT ACCOUNTS

We begin with the obvious—retirement savings vehicles. As you're aware, there are multiple ways to save for retirement. The main retirement account types are best categorized by their tax treatment.

TAXABLE ACCOUNTS

A taxable account is any account to which the IRS's standard tax rules and regulations apply, including brokerage accounts, other types of investment accounts, checking accounts, savings accounts, trusts, etc. We make contributions to these accounts with after-tax money. Contributions and income are unlimited, and withdrawals have no restrictions. The government taxes interest, dividends, and capital gains from taxable investments held within these accounts in the year they are realized.

When viewed from a retirement planning perspective, these accounts are beneficial because investment gains on shares held over twelve months are taxed at lower long-term capital gains rates which may be lower than ordinary income tax rates. In addition, these funds are readily available regardless of retirement status or age.

PRE-TAX ACCOUNTS

Pre-tax contributions to a retirement account lower your taxable income during the year in which you make them. The assets contributed are then free to grow in the account without tax implications until you withdraw them. ideally during retirement. Common types of pre-tax retirement accounts include IRAs, SIMPLE IRAs, SEP IRAs, 401(k)s, 403(b)s and 457s.

While pre-tax accounts offer the benefits of tax deferral, anytime you withdraw assets, they tax you at ordinary income rates on the amount withdrawn. In addition, if you receive a distribution from a pre-tax account before you have reached age 59½, you may be subject to a 10 percent early withdrawal penalty.

There is an exception for this rule that applies to 401(k)s. If you leave your company during the year in which you turn age fifty-five, or any year after that, and maintain your 401(k) account balance, you may be able to withdraw funds penalty free. This can be an important consideration, especially if you decide to retire from your primary career and move on to an encore career that's more fun and less stressful.

An important consideration with pre-tax accounts is that the IRS requires investors withdraw required minimum distributions (RMDs) from these accounts by April 1 following the year they turn age seventy-three or seventy-five (depending on when they were born), and by December 31 each year after, based on the current year's RMD calculation. Currently, for individuals born in 1959 or earlier, their RMD age is seventy-three. For individuals born in 1960 or after, their RMD age is seventy-five. This is an important factor to plan for, as you will be required to pay income taxes on the RMD amount each year.

TAX-FREE ACCOUNTS

In contrast to pre-tax accounts, individuals make contributions to tax-free accounts with after-tax funds. Although your taxable income does not decrease in the year you contribute, these accounts provide the advantage of tax-free growth within the account *and* tax-free withdrawals during retirement. Tax-free accounts include, but are not limited to, Roth IRAs, Roth 401(k) s, and Roth 403(b)s.

The tax-free withdrawals permitted by Roth accounts are a tremendous benefit for those living in retirement. And, because the IRS has already received its tax cut, it is unnecessary to take RMDs from tax-free accounts.

WHY TAX STATUS MATTERS

Why does the tax status of various account types matter? Aside from the immediate tax implications, having a variety of assets with different tax treatments provides flexibility and the opportunity to optimize your retirement income while potentially lowering your tax liabilities.

For example, some retirees begin their retirement in lower tax brackets, but after they reach age seventy-three/seventy-five and begin taking RMDs from their pre-tax accounts, they realize they will very likely never experience those lower tax brackets again.

A qualified wealth advisor can expect a future bump up in your tax bracket and help you take steps while you're still in a lower tax bracket to prepare for the upcoming increase. For instance, it may make sense to complete a Roth conversion of some of your pre-tax assets during a year in which you fall into a lower tax bracket. However, it's important to ensure you have enough liquid assets available to cover the required conversion taxes, rather than withhold the taxes from the conversion itself, which results in fewer net dollars to convert. These are just a few considerations your wealth advisor will discuss with you.

Another example applies specifically to retired corporate associates who have received company stock as compensation or who have purchased company stock over their career. If you hold a concentrated stock position that you would like to diversify, it may make sense to unwind your position while you fall into a lower long-term capital gains tax bracket.

ASSET LOCATION

After many years of working with corporate associates, I've found that most have "type-A" personalities. This is likely not a surprise to anyone. After all, type-A tendencies are often a prerequisite for the job. How does this impact retirement planning? Because of their need for order and predictability, many of my clients feel most comfortable when they allocate all of their retirement accounts in a similar manner and ensure consistent performance across the board. However, this approach can cause major harm to your portfolio returns and ultimately destroy your ability to successfully retire. Why? Because investing in this manner can be incredibly tax inefficient.

One very effective way to enhance the tax efficiency of a retirement portfolio is through a strategy called asset location, which can help minimize a portfolio's tax liability by allocating tax-efficient investments to taxable accounts and tax-inefficient investments to tax-advantaged accounts.

For example, assets invested in a Roth IRA can be withdrawn tax-free in retirement. It may not make sense to invest in tax-free bonds in a Roth account because those assets are already sheltered from taxes and don't require the additional protection. Instead, it probably makes more sense to invest in corporate bonds within the Roth account and hold the tax-free bonds in a taxable brokerage account.

The point is, asset location is important because it allows us to leverage the tax characteristics of all three retirement account types to their full potential. By purchasing a diversified mix of investments and allowing them to behave as they're supposed to, you have the potential to enhance your portfolio's returns while also minimizing your long-term tax liabilities.

For example, let's pretend David retires with $500,000 in a brokerage account and $500,000 in a pre-tax IRA. By placing assets such as tax-free bonds, treasury bonds, growth stocks, and companies that pay qualified dividends in his brokerage account, we may be able to significantly lower and control his taxes in any given year. We would then allocate corporate bonds, non-qualified dividend paying stocks and other ordinary income generating assets in his IRA. Since they would tax distributions from his IRA as ordinary income, there is less of a benefit in being tax efficient in that account.

It's important that asset location should be a secondary consideration to asset selection, and it's best to run this by your tax advisor. In addition, this strategy may need adjustment year over year based on your individual tax situation and projected lifetime taxes.

The most important takeaway here is that not all accounts should be identical in their investment mix, nor should they perform in lockstep. The goal is to optimize the *overall* performance of your portfolio while using unique characteristics of each account to lower your taxes over time.

TAX-EFFICIENT WITHDRAWAL STRATEGIES

Being intentional about how you draw down your retirement savings can help minimize your taxes in retirement, which is why it's important to have a tax-efficient withdrawal strategy in place *before* you retire. The good news is, if you've already implemented the asset location strategy noted above, you're likely invested in a variety of accounts with unique tax characteristics. This can be an advantage when planning your withdrawal strategy.

Three main withdrawal approaches should be considered. The one that's right for you depends on your retirement goals, monthly income needs, and overall tax situation.

1. **Traditional approach**—The traditional approach is to withdraw from one type of account at a time, beginning with taxable accounts, followed by tax-deferred accounts and, finally, tax-free accounts. This approach allows your tax-

advantaged savings to continue growing tax-deferred for a longer period. However, the challenge with this approach is that it greatly increases tax planning difficulty, as you will likely have significantly more taxable income in some years than others.

2. **Proportional approach**—Using a proportional approach, you establish a target percent that you plan to withdraw from each account each year. This amount is based on the proportion of your retirement savings held in each type of account. The benefit of this approach is that it helps ensure a more stable tax bill from one year to the next and can also help you save on taxes over time.

3. **Tax-bracket maximization approach**—If you're like many of my clients, it may be most tax efficient to first withdraw an amount to fill up your desired income tax bracket from pre-tax funds, then fill the rest of your monthly income needs with assets from your taxable accounts. This tax-planning strategy allows you to take advantage of filling up low-income tax brackets, control your taxable income, and maintain monthly/annual spending flexibility.

At Falcon Wealth Advisors, we discuss the pros and cons of all three strategies, with the caveat that we review and adjust our clients' withdrawal strategies on an annual basis and make adjustments as their life goals and situation develop over time. While some advisors take a "set-it-and-forget-it" approach to retirement withdrawals, we believe the best approach is rooted in well-established wisdom while also allowing enough flexibility to keep up with our clients' ever-evolving needs.

WHICH ACCOUNTS ARE RIGHT FOR ME?

As with so many financial considerations, the right mix of accounts for you depends on several factors, including your personal financial goals, retirement income needs, and tax situation. A retiree who falls into a higher tax bracket during her working years may choose to contribute to a pre-tax account to lower her taxes today, while someone who expects his taxes to be higher in retirement may choose to save in a Roth account.

Generally, it makes sense for most investors to save money in each of the three tax buckets, as this provides the benefit of tax diversification. If you have several accounts with different tax treatments, your advisor has flexibility in how to manage your taxes in retirement.

For example, perhaps you retire at age sixty-eight and begin taking regular withdrawals from your various accounts. Knowing that in five to seven years (at age seventy-three or seventy-five), you will need to take required minimum distributions, it may make sense to draw from your pre-tax accounts more during these early retirement years while you fall into a lower income tax bracket. Selecting an appropriate pre-tax withdrawal amount can help lower your future RMD responsibilities while still keeping you in a lower tax bracket.

SOCIAL SECURITY PLANNING

When planning for retirement, the decision about when to receive Social Security payments is important. The amount varies based on each individual's personal financial situation. Some people benefit from beginning payments as soon as possible, while others are better off delaying Social Security.

Facts about Social Security:

- Social Security was signed into law by President Franklin D. Roosevelt on August 14, 1935.[2]
- The first Social Security check was issued to Ida May Fuller on January 31, 1940, in the amount of $22.54.[3]
- In 2023, the average monthly Social Security check was roughly $1,837 per retired worker.[4]
- Today, Social Security is one of the largest government programs in the world, paying out more than one trillion dollars each year.[5]
- In 2023, an average of 67 million Americans received Social Security benefits each month, including nine out of ten people age sixty-five and older.[6]

Requirements for receiving Social Security:

- An individual must be at least age sixty-two and have paid into the program for a minimum of forty credits to be eligible for Social Security retirement benefits.
- They calculate the benefit based on an average of up to thirty-five years of a worker's indexed earnings. The Social Security Administration then applies a formula to calculate the primary insurance amount (PIA), which determines the amount of benefits an individual is eligible to receive.
- Assuming they meet certain requirements, spouses and

---

2   "Historical Background and Development of Social Security," Social Security Administration, accessed January 11, 2024, https://www.ssa.gov/history/briefhistory3.html.

3   "Historical Background and Development of Social Security."

4   "Fact Sheet: Social Security," Social Security Administration, accessed January 11, 2024, https://www.ssa.gov/news/press/factsheets/basicfact-alt.pdf.

5   "Fact Sheet: Social Security."

6   "Fact Sheet: Social Security."

ex-spouses may be entitled to a portion of an individual's Social Security benefits.

- The highest monthly benefit amount is available to those who wait until age seventy to receive payments.

SOCIAL SECURITY—AGE MATTERS

As an American taxpayer, you are eligible to receive Social Security payments as early as age sixty-two; however, full retirement benefits do not begin until you reach your full retirement age (FRA), also known as normal retirement age (NRA). FRA is based on the year in which you were born. For every year after FRA that you delay receiving benefits, you receive a higher benefit amount. After age seventy, the increase in benefits from delaying stops, so there is no reason to wait past age seventy to turn on benefits.

Your primary insurance amount (PIA) is the term used to describe the benefit you receive at FRA. You can calculate your particular PIA by creating an account on the Social Security Administration's website (https://www.ssa.gov/myaccount). This site is a great resource to help you gain an understanding of your projected benefit amounts and the difference in potential payments should you take benefits at age sixty-two versus age seventy.

If you elect to receive Social Security payments prior to your FRA, your benefit will be less than your PIA, which is a permanent reduction in your monthly payment. On the flip side, if you wait to receive payments until after your FRA, your benefit amount will be greater than your PIA, and this is a permanent increase in your monthly payment. Put simply, the amount you receive when you first take benefits is the amount you will receive for the rest of your life. That's one reason why timing is important.

The following table illustrates the difference in potential benefits based on age.

Effect of Early or Delayed Retirement on Retirement Benefits
Benefit, as a percentage of Primary Insurance Amount (PIA)

Year of Birth	Normal Retirement Age (NRA)	Credit for each year of delayed retirement after NRA (percent)	62	63	64	65	66	67	70
1924	65	3	80	86 2/3	93 1/3	100	103	106	115
1925–26	65	3 ½	80	86 2/3	93 1/3	100	103 ½	107	117 ½
1927–28	65	4	80	86 2/3	93 1/3	100	104	108	120
1929–30	65	4 ½	80	86 2/3	93 1/3	100	104 ½	109	122 ½
1931–32	65	5	80	86 2/3	93 1/3	100	105	110	125
1933–34	65	5 ½	80	86 2/3	93 1/3	100	105 ½	111	127 ½
1935–36	65	6	80	86 2/3	93 1/3	100	106	112	130
1937	65	6 ½	80	86 2/3	93 1/3	100	106 ½	113	132 ½
1938	65, 2 months	6 ½	79 1/6	85 5/9	92 2/9	98 8/9	105 5/12	111 11/12	131 5/12
1939	65, 4 months	7	78 1/3	84 4/9	91 1/9	97 7/9	104 2/3	111 2/3	132 2/3
1940	65, 6 months	7	77 ½	83 1/3	90	96 2/3	103 1/2	110 1/2	131 ½
1941	65, 8 months	7 ½	76 2/3	82 2/9	88 8/9	95 5/9	102 1/2	110	132 ½
1942	65, 10 months	7 ½	75 5/6	81 1/9	87 7/9	94 4/9	101 1/4	108 3/4	131 ¼
1943–54	66	8	75	80	86 2/3	93 1/3	100	108	132
1955	66, 2 months	8	74 1/6	79 1/6	85 5/9	92 2/9	98 8/9	106 2/3	130 2/3
1956	66, 4 months	8	73 1/3	78 1/3	84 4/9	91 1/9	97 7/9	105 1/3	129 1/3
1957	66, 6 months	8	72 ½	77 ½	83 1/3	90	96 2/3	104	128
1958	66, 8 months	8	71 2/3	76 2/3	82 2/9	88 8/9	95 5/9	102 2/3	126 2/3
1959	66, 10 months	8	70 5/6	75 5/6	81 1/9	87 7/9	94 4/9	101 1/3	125 1/3
1960 and later	67	8	70	75	80	86 2/3	93 1/3	100	124

Note: Persons born on January 1 of any year should refer to the previous year of birth.

Source: "Social Security Benefits: Effect of Early or Delayed Retirement Benefits," Social Security Online, Social Security Administration, accessed January 11, 2024, https://www.ssa.gov/OACT/ProgData/ar_drc.html.

WHEN IS THE BEST AGE TO RECEIVE PAYMENTS?

Your wealth advisor should be involved in the careful consideration of when to begin taking Social Security. Several factors must be considered, including the following.

Your Monthly Income Needs

One of the first pieces of information you need to establish is your monthly income requirements in retirement. This helps determine how much money you will need each month for living expenses. Your wealth advisor can help you develop a simple monthly budget to identify any income gaps you will need to fill.

Many former corporate associates discover they have enough retirement savings to fund their monthly income needs for several years, allowing them to delay Social Security. However, if you have gaps in your monthly income, it may make sense to take Social Security sooner rather than later.

Your Full Retirement Age

As noted in the previous table, the age at which you become eligible for full Social Security benefits is between sixty-five and sixty-seven, depending on the year you were born. If you claim early retirement benefits, you will trigger a permanent decrease in your monthly benefit amount, while initiating benefits after full retirement age will increase your monthly payment amount.

It's important to understand your full retirement age and how your decision of when to take benefits impacts your monthly benefit amount.

Your Life Expectancy

If you are healthy and have a family history of longevity, you may feel more confident delaying Social Security than someone who has a history of chronic disease, cancer, or obesity. Your life expectancy is an important consideration when determining Social Security timing.

YOUR MARITAL STATUS AND FAMILY SITUATION

If you are married, widowed, or divorced, you may be eligible to receive benefits based on your spouse's/ex-spouse's record and delay taking your own benefits until later.

The timing of your benefits may also impact the payments your spouse receives, should you pass away first. Because surviving spouses usually receive the higher of the spouses' two benefits, it sometimes makes sense for the higher-earning spouse to delay Social Security until full retirement age to maximize the amount received by the surviving spouse.

If you care for dependent children or parents, they may also be eligible to receive a portion of your Social Security after you pass away.

Your Income

If your combined income exceeds a certain threshold, your Social Security benefits may be subject to tax. Your combined income equals your adjusted gross income (AGI), plus non-taxable interest payments, plus half of your Social Security benefit. As your combined income increases, more of your Social Security benefit (up to 85 percent) is subject to income tax.

Also, depending on what state you live in, you may qualify for a state "tax break" on Social Security. Because my firm is headquartered in Kansas City, I'll use Missouri and Kansas as examples. Starting in 2024, in Missouri, Social Security is exempt from state income taxation. In Kansas, the total income threshold for this exemption is $75,000 or less.

Your Work Status

If you plan to pursue an encore career (see Chapter One), it's important to understand how your work income may impact your benefits. There are limits to how much you can earn between age sixty-two and your full retirement age and still receive your full Social Security benefit. They reduce your benefit by 50 percent for every dollar you make above the current limit. (In 2024, the annual earnings limit is $22,320.[7])

However, once you reach full retirement age, your earnings no longer impact your benefits, regardless of how much you earn. That's why it often makes sense for those who pursue encore careers to delay taking Social Security until FRA.

This rule has an exception for individuals who retire and receive Social Security benefits in the middle of the year. Under the special earnings limit rule, you may be eligible for your full Social Security benefit, even if you made more than the annual earnings limit prior to retiring, if you meet specific criteria.[8]

Also, once you reach FRA, they can recalculate your benefit if your Social Security benefit is reduced due to returning to work, to give you credit for the months when your payment was reduced. And, if you go back to work and earn more than the annual earnings limit, the IRS offers a one time opportunity to

7   "Receiving Benefits While Working," Social Security Administration, accessed January 11, 2024, https://www.ssa.gov/benefits/retirement/planner/whileworking.html.

8   "Special Earnings Limit Rule," Social Security Administration, accessed January 11, 2024, https://www.ssa.gov/benefits/retirement/planner/rule.html.

withdraw your Social Security benefit within twelve months of starting work. If you choose this option, you would need to pay back any benefits you received in the interim.

Your Investment Rate of Return

If your investments are earning a greater rate of return than the rate at which Social Security increases, you may take Social Security payments sooner than later. On the flip side, if your investments are earning less than the rate of Social Security increases, it may make more sense to postpone taking benefits.

Your Risk

At Falcon Wealth Advisors, we sometimes frame the decision of when to take Social Security in terms of what is safer or more conservative. For example, is it safer to receive payments at age sixty-two since Social Security benefits don't transfer to beneficiaries like retirement account assets do? Or, is it safer to delay taking Social Security until FRA to take advantage of the guaranteed benefit increase every year, which can be especially beneficial for someone who is concerned about outliving his or her assets?

The answer, like so many financial considerations, depends on your particular financial situation, life goals, and unique needs. Regardless, it's wise to consider risk as you're making your decision.

An experienced wealth advisor will help you navigate all the various complexities of Social Security timing in order to develop a course of action that's right for you based on your personal financial situation and retirement needs.

IS SOCIAL SECURITY A PONZI SCHEME?

Many people don't realize they sentenced Bernie Madoff to 150 years in prison for operating an investment business similar to Social Security. What do I mean by that? Social Security functions much like a Ponzi scheme because it uses new money to pay out original investors.

Many people mistakenly believe that the money deducted from their paycheck for Social Security is saved for their future benefits. Instead, those who are actively working are paying the benefits of those currently receiving Social Security payments. That means that future workers will fund your eventual benefits.

The problem is that transferring income from the current generation of workers to current retirees means we are reliant on the next generation to pay for retirement. Birth and labor rates have been slowing for decades. Coupled with the fact that baby boomers are currently retiring in droves, this is leading to a steady depletion of the Social Security trust fund.

So, is Social Security a Ponzi scheme? No, it's not in the technical sense, but it operates similarly. This "Ponzi-ish" approach to Social Security has many people worried about the program's long-term viability.

The main takeaway: planning for Social Security is important. However, it's not wise to heavily depend on Social Security benefits to fund your retirement. Saving for retirement in multiple accounts with varying tax treatments will provide you with the most flexibility to establish a monthly income stream and lower your taxes over time.

MAJOR PURCHASE PLANNING

Most people's retirement goals include making a major purchase or two. Maybe you have a dream of purchasing a second home on the beach, taking an extended trip to Europe, or purchasing an RV to tour the country. Whatever your goals may be, it's important to plan ahead. Work with your wealth advisor to answer the following questions prior to making a major purchase.

WHY DO I WANT TO MAKE THIS PURCHASE?

As we've discussed, it's important to consider the emotional side of your financial decisions. Start by asking yourself why you wish to make this major purchase and how it fits into your retirement priorities.

Perhaps you're on vacation in Florida and come across a real estate opportunity. Before jumping on it, make sure that doing so will get you closer to your main life goals/priorities, rather than farther away from them. Taking time to ask yourself, "Why do I want to make this purchase?" can help you determine if it's an impulse buy or one that will bring you happiness and fulfillment.

CAN I AFFORD TO MAKE THIS PURCHASE?

Once you decide this is a purchase in line with your priorities that will bring you closer to your retirement goals, you'll need to determine if your financial plan can handle the purchase. Another way to frame this question is, "How will making this purchase impact my overall financial situation?" or even, "Will I still be able to afford my desired retirement lifestyle?"

Work with your wealth advisor to model different scenarios to gauge the impact your purchase may have on your overall financial plan and future goals. If making the purchase is a priority, you may need to make some adjustments in other areas of your life to accommodate it.

Whatever you decide, make sure you have a full understanding of the impact the purchase will have on your financial plan and retirement lifestyle before jumping in.

SHOULD I PAY CASH OR BORROW?

If you decide to move forward with your purchase, the next question to ask yourself is, "How do I pay for it?" Your two main options are:

1. Pay up front using a lump sum of cash.
2. Finance your purchase and pay it off slowly over time.

Before making a decision, you should understand the terms of potential financing options, including:

- Length of loan
- Interest rate
- Payment terms
- Prepayment penalties

Many times, just knowing the terms of the financing can help you determine whether it makes sense to take a loan for your purchase. For example, if mortgage rates are high, it may make more sense to pay cash for your second home (assuming your financial plan allows).

As a general rule, if a loan's interest rate is lower than the average rate of return on your investments, it usually makes sense to borrow. If the loan's interest rate is more than what you're making on your investments, it may be more beneficial to make the purchase with cash.

It's also important to factor in your emotional reaction to the decision. Some clients are uncomfortable borrowing and would prefer to pay in cash, regardless of the circumstances. Others are uncomfortable seeing their investment portfolio drop by such a large amount and would prefer paying off a loan a little bit at a time.

Market conditions may impact your decision as well. If your account balance has increased because of a strong market, it may be a great time to take a distribution and pay cash for your major purchase. However, if your account balance is down, you may not want to sell and lock in that loss.

WHAT ACCOUNT(S) SHOULD I PULL FROM?

Regardless of whether you decide to pay cash or finance, you'll almost certainly need some cash in hand, at least for a down payment or home improvements/furnishings. So, the next question becomes, "From what account should I take a distribution?"

It's important to consider both the tax status of each account and its current rate of return. If you have liquid cash sitting in a checking or savings account, it may make sense to use those assets first so you don't have to disrupt your investments. Or, you may want to draw from several accounts based on their tax liabilities. If you're seventy-three/seventy-five or older, you may put your required minimum distribution (RMD) toward your purchase since you'll need to pay taxes on those assets, regardless.

Whatever decision you make, monitor how your distribution may affect your taxes for the year. You want to avoid moving up into a higher tax bracket. Your wealth advisor can implement forward tax planning strategies to help ensure your withdrawal is as tax-efficient as possible.

WHAT ABOUT UNPLANNED PURCHASES?

In this section, we talked a lot about planned purchases, but what about unplanned expenses? Unexpected major purchases come up all the time in retirement, such as a medical diagnosis or accident, the need to purchase a new car, a natural disaster that affects your home or other property, a lawsuit, etc.

If possible, it usually makes sense to draw from taxable accounts for unplanned expenses to avoid filling up your tax bracket. (For additional information, refer to "tax-bracket maximization approach" in the Tax-Efficient Withdrawal Strategies section.)

While it's impossible to plan for an unexpectedly enormous expense, all the same steps described above still apply. Collaborate with your wealth advisor to mitigate the effects of spontaneous expenses on your future goals.

WATCH OUT FOR DEPRECIATION

One last consideration to keep in mind is the future value of whatever item(s) you're purchasing. If you buy a home in a popular vacation area, it's possible you (or your heirs) can sell it for a profit in the future. However, if you purchase an RV, it's unlikely you will ever be able to sell it for the full amount you paid, because of depreciation. That means whatever money you used to purchase the RV is no longer available to grow in your portfolio, and will probably never be replaced.

TAX PLANNING

Taxes touch every aspect of your finances, from your daily purchases, to the amount of pay you receive from your paycheck, to your investment returns, to the amount you leave as a financial legacy for your loved ones. Taxes also have a HUGE impact on your ability to successfully retire. If you're not including tax minimization strategies in your financial plan, you could unknowingly reduce your retirement income by thousands of dollars each year.

In the next section, I cover several strategies that can help lower your taxes and optimize your retirement savings.

WITHDRAWAL STRATEGIES

The order in which you withdraw assets from your retirement savings can have a big impact on your taxes. If you're like many corporate associates, you probably have a variety of taxable and tax-advantaged accounts. It's crucial to carefully pull from each of these sources to manage your taxes in any given year.

I outlined several tax-efficient withdrawal strategies under the Optimizing Your Retirement Accounts part of this chapter. The key here is to reevaluate your distribution strategy annually. If you take a "set-it-and-forget-it" approach to retirement withdrawals, you could miss out on tax-saving opportunities.

Asset Location

I covered this topic more extensively in the Optimizing Your Retirement Accounts section, but it's worth restating here as well. Asset location refers to the strategy of lowering an individual's tax liability by putting different investments in accounts with varying tax treatments. Using this strategy, you would allocate tax-efficient investments to taxable accounts and tax-inefficient investments to tax-advantaged accounts.

As you're working to lower your tax liabilities, just remember that *where* you hold your assets can play a vital role in the amount of taxes you pay.

Net Unrealized Appreciation

Net Unrealized Appreciation (NUA) is a complex tax-planning strategy that involves taking a distribution of company stock from a 401(k) and putting that stock into a brokerage account rather than rolling it over. When done correctly in an appropriate situation, this strategy allows the investor to pay taxes at long-term capital gains rates on the appreciated stock, instead of being taxed at ordinary income rates.

Here's an example of how NUA can work.

John Taxpayer is sixty-two, married and has worked for Company A for many years. He has $3 million in his 401(k), $500,000 of which is invested in company stock. The cost basis on his employer's stock is $150,000 because it has greatly appreciated over time. We consider the remaining value of $350,000 as the NUA.

John retires and takes an in-kind distribution of the $500,000 worth of company stock. He rolls over the remaining $2,500,000 to an IRA. He pays ordinary income tax on the $150,000 cost basis, not the entire $500,000.

If John later sells the company stock, he would pay long-term capital gains tax on the $350,000 NUA, which is usually less than ordinary income tax rates.

If John rolls over his entire $3 million account balance to an IRA, then takes a $500,000 distribution from the stock, he will need to pay income tax on the full distribution at his ordinary tax rate. Not only is he likely paying higher taxes, this distribution may also push him into a higher tax bracket.

If you work at a publicly traded company and have company

stock in your 401(k), it may be worth having a conversation with your advisor about whether this strategy makes sense based on your particular financial situation.

Roth Conversion

A Roth conversion refers to the process of converting tax-deferred retirement assets to tax-free status. To do so, you must take a distribution from the pre-tax account (typically a traditional IRA or employer-sponsored 401(k)), pay taxes in the current year on the distributed amount, and move those assets into a Roth account. Once you hold the funds in the Roth IRA, they will continue to grow and you can withdraw them tax-free in retirement.

Roth conversions can be especially effective for corporate executives whose high incomes have prevented them from contributing to Roth accounts during their working years. However, because the amount converted is subject to ordinary income tax rates, it's important to be strategic in timing a Roth conversion.

In addition, it's important to note that after completing a Roth conversion, you may be subject to a five-year rule, which states that you cannot withdraw earnings tax-free for five years following the conversion.[9] For most taxpayers, this isn't a major issue because they don't plan to withdraw from the account for over five years, but it's an important restriction to be aware of.

Keep in mind that you have never paid taxes on the assets held in your pre-tax retirement accounts. However, if you know

---

9   There are exceptions to the five-year rule, including using the funds to cover: up to $10,000 toward the purchase of a first home, unreimbursed medical expenses that are greater than 10 percent of your adjusted gross income, health insurance premiums if you are unemployed, qualified higher education expenses for yourself or a family member, or an IRS tax levy. An exemption may also be available if you agree to accept annual periodic payments for five years or until you reach age 59 ½, whichever comes first. Also, the five-year rule does not apply to those age 59 ½ or older, disabled individuals, or the beneficiaries of a deceased owner.

anything about old Uncle Sam, it's that he's going to get his cut eventually. Completing a Roth conversion doesn't help you avoid taxes; it allows you to take control of the timing. That's why you must be strategic in determining when to complete a Roth conversion. If you firmly believe tax rates will be lower in the future, it doesn't make sense to complete a Roth conversion now.

Following are some guidelines to help determine whether a Roth conversion makes sense based on your personal financial decision.

Situations in which it may make sense to complete a Roth conversion:

- You experience a year in which your income is lower than normal (recent retirement, your spouse retired, etc.)
- You believe you will fall into a higher tax bracket in the future.
- You made a large charitable donation that reduced your taxable income.
- You wish to reduce the amount of your required minimum distributions (RMDs).
- You wish to leave a tax-free inheritance to your loved ones.

When NOT to complete a Roth conversion:

- The conversion will put you in a higher tax bracket for the year.
- You have high taxable investment gains.
- You expect to be in a lower tax bracket in future years.
- You don't have enough savings to pay the conversion tax. (It's generally more advantageous to pay the associated taxes from savings rather than reduce the amount of the Roth conversion.)
- You plan to leave your IRA to charity after you die. (Typically, it's better to donate appreciated securities, which you can pass along tax-free.)

- You will need the money within five years or less, as converted assets cannot be withdrawn without penalty during the five-year waiting period.
- You sold an investment, had higher-than-normal standard compensation, or received a large bonus or a deferred compensation payout. Any large income events have the potential to push you into a higher tax bracket, which likely makes it unwise to complete a Roth conversion.
- You are collecting Medicare and a Roth conversion would push you into a higher income category, resulting in higher monthly premiums.

Here's another important note. While it's impossible to predict where tax rates will be in the future, the tax reductions permitted by the Tax Cuts and Jobs Act (TCJA) of 2017 scheduled the tax reductions to revert to their original pre-TCJA levels on January 1, 2026, which could result in an increase to your tax rate. If you expect your income to be lower in the years leading up to 2026 (and later), it may make sense to administer a Roth conversion prior to this date.

As with all major tax planning moves, be sure to consult with your wealth advisor and tax preparer/accountant before taking action.

Charitable Giving

Following the Tax Cuts and Jobs Act of 2017, the high itemized standard deduction makes many people ineligible to write off charitable donations. Yet, various strategies exist that can reduce your taxes and increase the impact of your charitable contributions.

Donor-Advised Fund

A donor-advised fund (DAF) is a charitable fund that houses donations for current and future giving. The benefit of a DAF is that you can contribute sizably in the current year and receive the corresponding tax deduction, while being able to advise on the timing of distributions and the organizations where the donations are to be made.

For example, Jason and Tricia Smith decide to contribute $100,000 to a DAF. They can claim the full $100,000 as a charitable donation in the current year. The Smith's cannot access the money, but they can dictate the organizations that will receive donations and the timing of those donations.

It's important to note that adjusted gross income (AGI) limits apply regardless of whether you're gifting stock or cash to the DAF. The annual income tax deduction limit for contributions of non-cash assets is 30 percent of your AGI, and the deduction limit for cash is 60 percent of your AGI.

Qualified Charitable Distribution

As I've already noted, if you have assets in tax-deferred accounts, you will need to take required minimum distributions (RMDs) at age seventy-three/seventy-five. These RMDs are taxed at ordinary income tax rates, which can be a major liability for many former corporate associates.

One way to lower the tax liability of your RMD is to make a qualified charitable distribution (QCD) to a charity (or charities) of your choice. The IRS allows RMD-eligible individuals to donate up to $105,000 per year from a tax-deferred retirement account to a charity with no negative tax impact. The benefits of making a QCD include:

- QCDs maximize your charitable impact because they allow you to donate the full amount of your RMD directly to a charity, rather than taking a distribution to yourself, paying taxes, and donating a reduced amount.
- QCDs reduce your income tax liability because it does not include them in your taxable income for the year.
- QCDs allow taxpayers the flexibility of deciding whether to make one large donation or several smaller donations over the course of a year.
- QCDs can be made from more than one account type, including traditional IRAs, inherited IRAs, SEP IRAs, and SIMPLE IRAs.
- QCDs do not require you to file itemized taxes because they are excluded from your taxable income.
- QCDs have no impact on your adjusted gross income, which means you may be eligible for reduced Medicare premiums and lower Social Security tax rates.
- QCD limits are by individual, so a married couple filing jointly can together donate up to $210,000 per year as a QCD, as long as only $105,000 is contributed from a single spouse's account(s).

Direct Transfer of Appreciated Stock

Instead of selling out of a security, paying capital gains taxes and donating the remaining assets to charity, a direct transfer of appreciated stock can lower your tax liability and maximize your charitable impact. That's a win/win for both you and the charitable organization.

Transferring appreciated securities straight to a charity can help lower your taxes because:

- You receive a charitable deduction for the current market value of the stock.
- The direct transfer of stock to a 501(c)(3) organization does not trigger capital gains taxes for either you or the charity.
- The charity receives the full value of the appreciated stock.

On the flip side, if you're considering donating a stock that has decreased in value, it might be more advantageous to sell it and use the loss to offset the tax implications of gains elsewhere in your portfolio, then donate the cash from the sale.

Health Savings Accounts

Health Savings Accounts (HSAs) provide a great opportunity to lower your taxes and save for future health-related expenses. In fact, HSAs are perhaps the most tax-efficient savings vehicle available, as they allow for triple tax advantages.

1. Because contributions are made with pre-tax dollars, they reduce your taxable income in the current year.
2. HSA funds grow tax deferred in the account.
3. When used to pay for eligible medical expenses, HSA withdrawals are tax-free.

Once an individual reaches age sixty-five, they can withdraw and use HSA funds for any purpose. However, taxes would apply to any funds used for non-medical-related expenses.

HSA contributions made via payroll deduction are not subject to Social Security or Medicare taxes. And, unlike other pre-tax retirement plans, HSA accounts are not subject to required minimum distributions.

For 2024, the IRS allows individuals to contribute up to $4,150 to an HSA ($8,300 per family). Those age fifty-five and older can make an additional $1,000 catch-up contribution. HSAs allow you to change your contribution amount at any time, not only when a qualifying life event occurs. Any unused funds automatically roll over to the next year, which allows these plans to essentially function as emergency savings vehicles.

One caveat to HSAs is that you must be enrolled in a high-deductible health insurance plan to establish and fund an account.

Tax-Loss Harvesting

Tax-loss harvesting involves selling an investment that has declined in value and replacing it with a highly correlated alternative. This allows you to realize an investment loss that can offset gains and lower your tax liability. When done correctly, the risk profile and expected return of your portfolio remain unchanged.

However, if done incorrectly, tax-loss harvesting can trigger the wash-sale rule, which occurs when an investor sells a security at a loss and, within thirty days before or after the sale, buys a substantially identical security. If the IRS deems the transaction a wash sale, you are not eligible for the investment loss or the associated tax savings. Therefore, it's important to only attempt tax-loss harvesting with the guidance of a qualified wealth advisor.

It's also important that you should never invest with the intent to sell an investment at a loss. It's not wise to miss out on the upside of investments solely to avoid taxes. Your primary strategy should always be to achieve investment gains within your portfolio. However, sometimes losses are inevitable, and that's when it may make sense to consider tax-loss harvesting opportunities.

CHAPTER THREE

Healthcare, Insurance, and Estate Planning

HEALTHCARE PLANNING

Health care expenses are among the largest costs faced by retirees. In fact, according to a Fidelity Retiree Health Care Cost Estimate, an average retired couple age sixty-five in 2023 can expect to pay roughly $315,000 in healthcare expenses over the course of their retirement.[10] That statistic alone illustrates how important it is to plan for retirement healthcare expenses.

THE IMPORTANCE OF INSURANCE

The first step in planning for healthcare expenses in retirement is selecting insurance coverage that meets your specific needs. Ideally, healthcare planning should begin *before* you retire, which is

---

10   "How to Plan for Rising Health Care Costs," Fidelity Viewpoints, Fidelity, June 21, 2023, https://www.fidelity.com/viewpoints/personal-finance/plan-for-rising-health-care-costs.

why I'm going to frame the conversation by age—younger than sixty-five and age sixty-five or older.

HEALTHCARE INSURANCE—YOUNGER THAN SIXTY-FIVE

If you have not yet reached age sixty-five and are working for an employer that provides an affordable health insurance plan (and that plan meets your needs), it probably makes sense to stick with your employer-sponsored coverage while you can. Employers often help cover the costs of premiums, which can make these plans affordable for most employees.

If your employer does not offer healthcare insurance, you can purchase your own policy at healthcare.gov, the national healthcare exchange. The site allows you to enter some basic information about yourself and compare multiple health insurance options. You can also enroll in coverage on the site during the annual open enrollment period, which typically runs from early November through mid-January.

Plans on the national exchange must meet the requirements of the Affordable Care Act and provide coverage for ten essential benefit categories (including coverage for preexisting conditions). One advantage of enrolling in a healthcare plan through the national exchange is that you may qualify for a health insurance subsidy. For 2021 through 2025, there's no longer an income cap to qualify for healthcare insurance subsidies. That means even a couple making more than $200,000 per year can still qualify. The maximum any individual will pay for health insurance coverage through the exchange is 8.5 percent of his or her income.

If you have access to employer-sponsored healthcare insurance that is *not* affordable for the rest of your family (costing 9.1 percent or more of your household income), you may qualify for a subsidized plan through healthcare.gov. This provision helps make insurance more affordable for more families.

HEALTHCARE INSURANCE—AGE SIXTY-FIVE AND OLDER

Once you reach age sixty-five, you are eligible for Medicare, the federal health insurance program for older Americans. Medicare comprises four parts, which all cover specific benefits and vary in cost.

1. **Medicare Part A, hospital insurance**—Part A covers the cost of inpatient hospitalizations, skilled nursing facilities, hospice care, and certain home healthcare costs. If you or your spouse has paid Medicare taxes for over ten years (forty quarters), there are typically no costs associated with Part A coverage. If you don't qualify for premium-free Part A, you may purchase coverage. In 2024, the standard Part A premium for an individual who has paid Medicare taxes for fewer than thirty quarters is $505 per month. For individuals who have paid into Medicare for thirty to thirty-nine quarters, the standard premium is $278 per month.[11]

2. **Medicare Part B, medical insurance**—Part B is the medical insurance portion of Medicare. It covers doctors' services, outpatient care, diagnostic testing, medical supplies, and preventative services. Everyone pays a monthly premium for Part B, and most people pay the standard premium, which in 2024 is $174.70 per month.[12] If your modified adjusted

---

11   "2023 Medicare Parts A & B Premiums and Deductibles 2023 Medicare Part D
Income-Related Monthly Adjustment Amounts," Fact sheet, Centers for Medicare
& Medicaid Services (CMS), September 27, 2022, https://www.cms.gov/newsroom/
fact-sheets/2023-medicare-parts-b-premiums-and-deductibles-2023-medicare-part-d-income-related-monthly.

12   "2023 Medicare Parts A & B Premiums and Deductibles," CMS.

gross income is more than a certain amount, you will pay the standard premium amount plus an Income-Related Monthly Adjustment Amount (IRMAA). For individuals with a modified AGI of more than $500,000, the maximum IRMAA is $419.30 per month in 2024 (for a total premium amount of $594 per month).

3. **Medicare Part C, Medicare Advantage Plan**—Medicare Advantage is a Medicare-approved private health insurance plan that serves as an alternative to original Medicare. These plans typically offer bundled coverage, including Part A, Part B, and Part D. Plans may also offer additional benefits that Medicare does not, including vision, hearing, and dental coverage.

Each Medicare Advantage Plan has different out-of-pocket expenses, so it's important to find a plan that both meets your needs and fits within your budget.

4. **Medicare Part D, prescription drug coverage**—Part D helps cover the cost of prescription drugs, shots and vaccines. To receive Part D coverage, you must join a Medicare-approved plan that offers prescription drug coverage. Part D plans have different monthly premiums based on the level of coverage you select. Plans also differ in what specific drugs they cover, so it's important to closely evaluate your options and select a plan that covers your medications. It's also important to note that, while enrolling in a Part D plan is optional, the government may impose a cumulative penalty for every month you don't have coverage. This penalty is applied to the premium of any Part D plan you may decide to enroll in at some point in the future.

Note—If you have reached age sixty-five, are still working and have credible employer-sponsored health insurance, you are not required to enroll in Medicare.

There are many considerations to keep in mind as you evaluate your retirement health insurance options. I strongly recommend working with an experienced insurance broker who is well-versed in Medicare's many provisions and can help you select options that make sense for your personal financial situation.

PAYING FOR HEALTHCARE IN RETIREMENT
HEALTH SAVINGS ACCOUNTS

Now that I've summarized your health insurance options in retirement, you may wonder, "How will I pay for it all?" A great way to save for retirement healthcare expenses is through a Health Savings Account (HSA).

HSAs have grown in popularity over the last few years because of their tax-efficient nature. These accounts offset the expenses of qualified high-deductible healthcare plans while you're working, but they're also a great retirement savings vehicle.

To make HSA contributions, you must meet the following requirements.

- You are covered under a high-deductible health plan (HDHP) on the first day of the month.
- You have no other health insurance coverage.
- You are not enrolled in Medicare.
- You cannot be claimed as a dependent on someone else's tax return.[13]

---

13 "Publication 969 (2022), Health Savings Accounts and Other Tax-Favored Health Plans," Internal Revenue Service (IRS), updated February 1, 2023, https://www.irs.gov/publications/p969#en_US_2021_publink1000204025.

Assuming you meet the eligibility requirements, the 2024 IRS HSA contribution limit is $4,150 per individual, or $8,300 per family. Those age fifty-five and older are eligible to make an additional $1,000 catch-up contribution. Money contributed to an HSA is tax advantaged in three ways:

1. Because contributions are made with pre-tax dollars, they reduce your taxable income in the year they are made.
2. HSA funds grow tax-free in the account.
3. When used to pay for eligible medical expenses, HSA withdrawals are tax-free.

Additional benefits of saving in an HSA include:

- HSA contributions made via payroll deduction are not subject to Social Security or Medicare taxes.
- Unlike 401(k)s and other tax-deferred retirement savings accounts, HSAs are not subject to required minimum distributions (RMDs).
- Once you meet certain asset minimums, you can invest your HSA funds, which will provide the potential for growth over time and further enhance your retirement savings.
- When you reach age sixty-five, you can take penalty-free distributions from the HSA for non-medical expenses. (Distributions for non-medical expenses are still treated as ordinary income, much like an IRA distribution.)
- If you make payroll deferrals to your HSA, you have the flexibility to change your contribution amount at any time, not only when a qualifying life event occurs.
- Any contributions to an HSA automatically roll over to the next year, unlike a flexible spending account (FSA), which requires you to forfeit any unused funds at the end of the year.

- HSAs allow you the flexibility to pay for current medical expenses out of pocket and receive a future tax-free distribution to cover the expenses. This means you can treat the account as an emergency savings vehicle, only withdrawing funds when absolutely necessary. (Just be sure to save all medical receipts so you can claim reimbursement in the future.)
- HSA funds are fully portable, so you own the account and can take it with you when you retire or change employers. The money in your HSA remains available to pay for your medical expenses, regardless of where you work or when you stop working.

OTHER WAYS TO SAVE FOR HEALTHCARE EXPENSES

While HSAs are a tax-efficient way to save for healthcare expenses in retirement, their eligibility requirements mean they're not available to everyone. If you're not eligible to contribute to an HSA, consider saving for retirement healthcare expenses in a traditional or Roth IRA. (Refer to the Optimizing Your Retirement Accounts section in Chapter Two for more information.)

In the years leading up to retirement, it's also wise to establish a robust short-term emergency fund to cover any unexpected expenses that may come up. You should plan to have at least three to six months of living expenses set aside for emergency use. Keeping funds readily accessible in a savings account can help you avoid selling out of investments at inopportune times. Any time you tap into your emergency savings for unexpected medical expenses, or any other purchase, be sure to replace those funds as soon as possible so they're there when you need them.

RISK MANAGEMENT: WHAT INSURANCE DO YOU NEED?

Now that you've done the work to build your wealth, it's absolutely vital that you protect it. Without the proper insurance in place, your nest egg is at risk. None of us can predict what the future will hold, which is why it's important to be prepared. In this section, we cover the basic insurance policies you should consider in retirement.

MEDICAL INSURANCE

Medical insurance is arguably the most important type of policy to carry throughout retirement, as unexpected healthcare-related expenses can quickly erode your retirement savings if not properly planned for.

Medicare coverage is available for most individuals aged sixty-five and older. However, it's essential you have a policy in place prior to this age if you retire early. If you are exceptionally healthy and have few annual medical expenses, consider a high-deductible medical plan. If this is the right choice for you, you may have the added benefit of contributing to a health savings account (HSA). (For information regarding the benefits of an HSA, refer to information about Tax Planning included earlier in this chapter.) If you have health issues that require frequent doctor visits, it may make more sense to choose an HMO or PPO option.

Sources for insurance include COBRA and the secondary health insurance market. As with all financial decisions, it's important to work with a qualified professional who can help you evaluate your options and choose a policy that meets your specific needs.

LIFE INSURANCE

Life insurance is an important part of any financial plan because it protects your loved ones should you die unexpectedly. Life insurance requires that you pay a premium to cover a specified death benefit. Your premium is determined by the amount of the death benefit, your age, and your current level of health.

Life insurance policies are typically most important during an individual's working years, especially if the insured is the family's primary breadwinner. While there may be specific circumstances in which it makes sense to carry life insurance in retirement, it's important to carefully weigh the pros and cons prior to purchasing a policy. Most times, there are more efficient ways to protect your loved ones once you've retired.

That said, one situation in which it does often make sense to purchase life insurance in retirement is if you intend to take a single life annuity payout from your pension plan. Here, if you suddenly pass away, your family would not receive any additional monthly payments from the pension.

For example, upon retiring, you decide to take a portion of your pension as a single life annuity and receive a payment of $500 per month. You also decide to purchase a life insurance policy with a payout equal to an amount that if invested could earn approximately $500 per month or close to $500 per month, so your family receives some monthly income should you die unexpectedly. This life insurance policy provides additional protection for those who rely on your monthly pension income. It's important to note that there is risk associated with either strategy and this should be discussed with your wealth advisor.

LONG-TERM CARE INSURANCE

Traditional medical insurance and Medicare rarely cover the expense of extended care in a nursing home or long-term care facility. A long-term care policy can pay the expenses of extended care if you become unable to perform certain daily living activities, such as eating, bathing, using the restroom, etc.

Long-term care insurance helps manage longevity risk by protecting your assets should you require full-time care help. These policies normally require you to pay a monthly premium or one time lump sum for long-term care coverage.

Traditional long-term care policies take a "use-it-or-lose-it" approach to providing benefits, meaning that if you don't need long-term care during your lifetime, you lose the amount you've paid in premiums throughout the years. Today, several types of hybrid policies are available, for example, a whole life insurance policy with a long-term care rider. You must be extremely careful with these types of policies, as there are often high hidden fees. Whenever multiple products are combined in this manner, each product has its own expenses that can quickly add up.

It's also important to know that insurance companies can change the terms of your long-term policy along the way, which can erode any potential benefit you may receive. And remember that the insurance company selling you your long-term care policy is in the business of making money. The insurance provider is betting that you will pay lots of money in premiums and never draw from the benefits. You'ree buying a product that's designed for the insurance company's benefit, not yours.

My thought regarding long-term care insurance is that it should almost always be a last resort. If you have enough assets to cover the cost of long-term care, it's usually better to go that route rather than pay high premiums for a policy you may never need.

DISABILITY INSURANCE

Disability insurance can provide an income stream should you become unable to work because of an injury or illness. It may make sense to have a disability insurance policy in place if you continue to depend on income from a job in the years leading up to retirement, especially if you work in a high-risk position.

There are several types of disability coverage available, so it's important to choose a policy that's right for your specific needs. If you leave your corporate job to start your own business in the years leading up to retirement, consider an "own occupation" policy to provide a benefit should you become disabled and can no longer perform the functions of your job.

For example, let's assume Martha is an IT Professional who writes code for a large company. Writing code may require her to have use of her hands to operate a keyboard and mouse. If Martha develops a random case of severe arthritis and is unable to type, having an "own occupation" policy may provide her compensation while she seeks treatment.

PROPERTY AND CASUALTY INSURANCE

There are several types of property/casualty insurance you should consider carrying throughout retirement.

- **Homeowner's insurance**—I typically recommend you maintain at least enough coverage to account for 80 percent of your home's replacement cost. One hundred percent replacement coverage is most prudent, if it makes sense, given your overall financial situation. When considering your coverage amount, it's important to include items of value such as jewelry, artwork, collectibles, etc.
- **Car insurance**—Maintaining an adequate level of auto lia-

bility insurance is especially important for high-net-worth individuals. If you drive a luxury car and are involved in an accident that results in injury, your chance of being sued is dramatically higher than someone with a less expensive car. A common policy may be $100,000 of coverage per individual with $300,000 maximum liability coverage per accident and $100,000 of property damage coverage. Of course, the exact amount of coverage varies based on your car type and overall financial situation.

- **Umbrella insurance**—An umbrella policy provides additional protection above your homeowner's and car insurance, typically one million dollars to several million dollars in coverage. It's smart to have an umbrella policy in place to protect you with a car accident, or an accident on your property, or a lawsuit.

I recommend clients undertake an annual insurance review with their insurance agent or wealth advisor to help ensure their coverage remains adequate to cover their risks while also making sure they're not overpaying for insurance they no longer need.

Annuities

Annuities are a type of insurance policy designed to provide a lifetime stream of income in retirement. In exchange for either a lump sum payment or monthly premium, you are guaranteed monthly income payments once you retire. Annuity providers often tout the benefit of receiving, "monthly income you can't outlive!" Sounds like a great deal, right? Not so fast.

Annuities have the potential to provide great benefits—to the insurance companies that sell them. They are most definitely NOT in the best interest of most investors. Why? The answer is simple—

fees, fees, and more fees. Before you even see a penny, you have paid fees to the insurance company, the "advisor" who sold you the product (who, by the way, is likely not required to act in your best interest), and the investment manager managing the funds.

Not only that, but your assets become locked up once they are invested in an annuity product. You typically cannot withdraw your premiums without paying hefty surrender fees, ordinary income taxes, and possibly even a 10 percent early withdrawal penalty. This can be a big problem if you experience a change in your lifestyle that requires you to access those funds.

Also, annuities do not receive a step-up in cost basis when inherited, which may cause significant tax implications for your loved ones.

Instead of purchasing an annuity, you're almost always better off investing in a diversified mix of stocks, bonds, and options, while also maintaining an allocation to cash and treasury bonds to fund your short-term income needs.

LEGACY AND ESTATE PLANNING

Estate planning is a vital component of any retiree's financial plan. Not only does proper estate planning ensure your assets are passed along according to your wishes, it also helps prevent conflict among family members and allows your loved ones to avoid the very slow, expensive, and stressful probate process.

Estate planning is an important task for everyone to undertake, regardless of assets or financial complexity. If you don't have a proper estate plan in place, you may put your loved ones at risk.

In this section, I cover the basic estate planning documents you should consider implementing. An estate planning attorney can help you develop a custom estate plan that meets your specific needs.

WILLS AND TRUSTS

Many clients often confuse the difference between a will and a trust. While both documents are used to designate who should receive your assets after you die, there are some important differences to be aware of.

Probate

A will is a document that is filed in probate court after you pass away. I consider it your "voice" in probate court because it specifies how you'd like your assets to be distributed. However, it does not completely avoid the probate process, which can be extremely costly, time consuming, and overwhelmingly stressful for your family members.

In addition, probate is a public process, so your heirs are a matter of public record and may be targeted by salespeople and unscrupulous financial "advisors" who wish to share in their fortune.

Many people prefer to avoid the probate process all together, which is where a trust comes in. A trust is a private narrative document that specifies precisely how your assets should be passed along under multiple different circumstances. It allows for the direct transfer of assets without outside influence and public scrutiny.

Taxes

How taxes are handled is another important consideration when choosing between wills and trusts. When you die without a trust, there are multiple levels of taxes your heirs may need to pay, potentially including local probate taxes, federal estate taxes, and even state estate taxes. While many of these taxes are completely avoidable, thanks to the current high federal estate tax exemption ($13.61 million per individual, $27.22 million per married couple filing jointly, for people who pass away in 2024), there's no guarantee that the exemption won't be lowered again in the future or that your future earnings won't push you above the threshold.

Having a trust in place may allow for simpler tax planning than a will.

Titling Assets

A downside to using a trust is the added responsibility of retitling assets. For a trust to be effective, it must own assets, which means it's important to retitle all assets and accounts in the trust's name. This can be a major undertaking.

With just a will in place, assets can stay in your name until you die, at which point it becomes the job of the executor to retitle assets under your estate. Note, however, that even with a will in place, it's important to designate beneficiaries for each of your accounts and assets.

Smooth Transition

A trust specifies a successor trustee to manage your finances following your death, which can help ensure a smooth transition of assets to your heirs in a straightforward and timely manner. In contrast, wills can take months or years to process, and it forces your heirs to go through the probate process.

While the benefits of establishing a trust may seem to greatly outweigh a will, there are circumstances under which it can make more sense to have a will instead. Some people don't need all the bells and whistles of a trust and may choose to use a simple will to protect any assets that need to go through probate. You can avoid probate on an asset-by-asset basis by accurately naming beneficiaries to all accounts, including investment accounts, life insurance, checking and savings accounts, your vehicle(s), etc.

You can also bypass probate with certain designations and deed work. For example, you can establish a beneficiary deed to automatically transfer your home to your children and avoid probate following the death of the second spousal homeowner.

The decision to implement a will or a trust is a deeply personal one that depends on your goals, financial situation, legacy wishes, tax situation, and more. It's important to consult with a qualified estate planning attorney to determine which type of document is right for you.

OTHER IMPORTANT ESTATE PLANNING DOCUMENTS

Besides a will or trust, it's important to have the following estate planning documents in place.

- **Guardianship designations**—While it's common for guardianship designations to be included within a will or trust, the importance of making this declaration is enough for me to call it out on its own. If you don't officially designate who will care for your children following your death, a court may grant custody to someone you would not have chosen.
- **Durable power of attorney**—This legal document designates an individual to act on your behalf should you become incapacitated and unable to make financial decisions on your own.
- **Healthcare power of attorney**—Similar to a durable power of attorney, a healthcare power of attorney designates an individual to make medical decisions on your behalf should you become incapacitated and unable to do so on your own.
- **Advanced healthcare directive**—This document stipulates

what medical treatments you wish to receive, should you become unable to express these wishes on your own. It can also state any life-saving methods you wish to avoid.

- **Letter of intent**—While not a legally binding document, a letter of intent can be a helpful way to inform your executor, beneficiary, or the court of your intentions. People sometimes use these letters to express their funeral wishes or designate how a special asset/possession should be handled.
- **Special needs trust**—If you care for a loved one with special needs, you may wish to establish a special needs trust to help cover ongoing care. When implemented effectively, a special needs trust can provide support for your loved one without disqualifying him/her from receiving Supplemental Security Income (SSI).

THE DO'S AND DON'TS OF ESTATE PLANNING

Following are some important do's and don'ts to follow as you plan for your estate.

Do...

- Work with a qualified estate planning attorney.
- Ensure your estate plan is in line with your overall financial plan and long-term objectives.
- Put powers of attorney in place. Powers of attorney are powerful documents that dictate who can make decisions on your behalf.
- Designate beneficiaries on all accounts and assets.
- Review your estate plan regularly—at least every five years and anytime you experience a major life event.
- Be transparent and upfront with your loved ones. Share your estate planning attorney's contact information with your ben-

eficiaries so they know who to contact should you suddenly die. Consider sharing your plans with your family members so they understand your wishes and know what to expect.

Don't…

- Assume that the default in the absence of doing something is what you would want to happen. The state will dictate what happens if you don't specify, which may not be what you would have chosen.
- Let imperfection keep you from drafting an estate plan. The best you can do is choose options that make sense in the present. You can always make changes as your life and circumstances evolve over time. Don't let the fear of making a mistake delay the process.
- Procrastinate. You never know when your estate plan may become essential.
- Forget to designate a legal guardian for your children.
- Fail to name beneficiaries for items of significance, such as jewelry, artwork, and collectibles.
- Forget to plan for life insurance, retirement accounts, and investment accounts.

I think that covers the core financial planning issues you need in place to retire right. Of course, there are many more complexities that go into each of these considerations, which is why it's always important to work with a wealth advisor. Once you have a detailed financial plan in place, you're well on your way toward achieving financial security in retirement!

CHAPTER FOUR

Investment Management

Okay, we're making progress! You've decided that you're mentally and psychologically ready to retire and you've done the financial planning work to make that happen. The next thing you need to ask yourself is, "Am I invested appropriately?"

This is an important question, as any missteps here could cost you thousands, if not millions, of dollars over the course of your retirement. Remember that retirement is not the finish line; it's the beginning of a new stage of life. While your investment objectives in retirement will shift, they don't stop entirely.

In this chapter, I'll cover the basics of investment management in retirement. However, as with so many critical financial decisions, it's wise to seek the advice of a wealth advisor who can help keep you on track toward your unique retirement goals.

HOW TO INVEST FOR SUCCESS IN RETIREMENT

Over many years of helping clients retire, I've found that many people hold misconceptions about investing in retirement. They often think the best approach is to park their assets in a savings account or a stable value fund to protect them from market volatility. This can be a HUGE mistake!

For example, let's assume Nelly is scared of the stock market and doesn't trust the government or anyone else. She decides to park her entire retirement fund of $1,000,000 into a savings account yielding less than 3 percent. If Nelly spends $75,000 per year she could reasonably expect to deplete her account within eighteen years. However if Nelly diversifies her holdings and earns an average return of 6 percent, her funds would last her close to twenty-eight years. All by diversifying between stocks and bonds! There are obviously no guarantees. By letting your biases influence your investment decisions, you run the risk of making costly mistakes.

While it's true that a portion of your portfolio should be available to cover short-term living expenses, it's vital to continue seeking growth as well. Remember that many people's retirement savings must last for twenty, thirty, or even forty years. Even if you have enough assets to last a lifetime, it may significantly deplete your purchasing power if they do not keep up with inflation.

When investing in retirement, it's important to focus on two major objectives.

OBJECTIVE #1—GROWTH OF ASSETS TO LAST A LIFETIME

I typically recommend that clients invest a portion of their assets in a diversified portfolio focused on growth, which also provides inflation protection. I believe one of the most effective ways to help provide growth and protect against inflation is by purchasing stock in companies. This allows your assets to grow alongside the companies' earnings.

OBJECTIVE #2—SHORT-TERM ACCESS TO LIQUID CAPITAL TO COVER MONTHLY INCOME NEEDS

Besides growth assets, most every retiree needs access to liquid capital to cover everyday living expenses. Based on your specific goals (as outlined in your financial plan), you may need to maintain anywhere from five to ten years' worth of living expenses in a cash or cash-equivalent account.

This account helps protect your growth assets, as it prevents you from needing to sell out of the market at inopportune times. It also allows you to live your life without worrying about the day-to-day fluctuations in the stock market.

Remember that emotional component to retirement we discussed in Chapter One? That comes into play here, as well. It can be very difficult for some retirees to realize the income they received from a paycheck for many years is no longer there. Having a plan in place to cover your monthly expenses, while also growing your assets for future use, can provide a level of calmness in retirement.

WHAT IS MY IDEAL RETIREMENT ALLOCATION?

Your ideal retirement investment allocation will be heavily driven by your specific cash flow needs. Your monthly income requirements are unique and must be met by an appropriate, steady stream of income.

Remember that no two clients' allocations will be absolutely alike. For example, based on this financial plan, goals, and other sources of income, John Client may need to withdraw $10,000 per month from his retirement savings to fund his lifestyle, while Jane Client may only need $5,000 per month. Therefore, John may need to allocate more assets to fixed income or other liquid investments than Jane.

As a starting point, I would recommend that John allocate a minimum of $600,000 to bonds and other liquid assets to cover five years of living expenses ($10,000 × 12 months = $120,000, $120,000 × 5 years = $600,000). Jane would only need to allocate $300,000 of her retirement assets to cover her living expenses for five years ($5,000 × 12 months = $60,000, $60,000 × 5 years = $300,000).

As I mentioned above, I typically advise clients to have between five and ten years of living expenses invested conservatively outside of the stock market. Why five to ten years? Because the average market cycle is roughly five years. This means, if you have five to ten years' worth of savings invested outside of the stock market, your stock portfolio should be well positioned to withstand one to two full market cycles without any disruption during a downturn.

As you systematically withdraw from your short-term funds, look for opportunities to shift some assets from your stock portfolio to your short-term allocation in a tax-efficient manner during favorable times in the market cycle. This allows you to continue funding your cash flow needs while also maximizing growth in your stock portfolio.

Regarding your short-term account, I strongly favor a healthy allocation to bonds in this portion of the portfolio. While bonds are subject to some volatility, especially when compared to a money market or other stable assets, they often have the added benefit of generating income as regular interest payments. Investment-grade bonds, in particular, can be especially effective in this portion of the portfolio because they typically are less volatile than stocks and pay out interest. (We'll come back to this topic later.)

Okay, let's break things up a bit. Unless you're relying on this book to put you to sleep tonight, it may be helpful to summarize a few retirement investing tips, rather than going into all the details. So, here you have it—the do's and don'ts of investing for success in retirement.

Do...

- **Regularly review your financial plan and investment allocation with a wealth advisor**—It's vital to periodically review your plan and investments to ensure they continue to keep up with your ever-evolving life and goals. If you're nervous about something happening in your portfolio or the markets, talk to your advisor. If you have a question, no matter how small, talk to your advisor. If you would like to review something, talk to your advisor. Remember, it's your future at stake. You have a right to know the details of your financial plan and investment allocation.

- **Recognize that investing for retirement will look different at age sixty than at age eighty**—Even if your goals never change with time (which they will), your needs will. Investing for retirement is not a "set-it-and-forget-it" task. Your portfolio allocation should evolve over time, just as you do.

- **Remain flexible**—Understand that a financial plan is not a set roadmap. Life is dynamic. Markets are dynamic. Your goals are dynamic. The minute you create a financial plan, it's already outdated because so many variables are influencing it every day. It's okay. It doesn't have to be perfect. An imperfect plan is better than no plan at all. Define your investing success as a trajectory, not just a final number. Are you moving in the right direction? If yes, great! You'll still need to make some changes and tweaks as your life evolves. It's all part of the process.

Don't…

- **Think that retirement is the finish line**—Remember that retiring is only the beginning, not the end. Don't park all of your assets in a stable value fund and expect success. Instead, make wise investment decisions that will help ensure your assets are available to support your lifestyle over the next two, three, or even four decades.
- **Think there's a cookie-cutter way to invest for retirement**—Remember, you should tailor your investment strategy to yourself, your financial situation, and your goals for the future, not anyone else's. Don't worry about what your neighbor, golf buddy, or brother-in-law are doing. Focus on investing for the future *you* hope to live in.
- **Tie your self-worth to your net worth**—As you progress through life in retirement, you will likely spend down some of your assets. It's natural that you could have fewer assets ten years from now than you do today. It may not be easy to go from saving your whole life to spending, and it's normal to feel uneasy as your portfolio value drops over time. However, it's also important to give yourself permission to live your life. Unless you have goals of maintaining your portfolio as a financial legacy, don't be so concerned about preserving your assets that you miss out on opportunities to enjoy your wealth.

CAN'T I DO THIS ON MY OWN?

Investing isn't rocket science. Anyone can technically buy and sell stocks. And, with all the information at our fingertips these days, it's easier than ever to access a virtually unlimited universe of research, insights, stock tips, etc. So, when someone asks me, "Can't I just do this on my own?" my answer is, "Yes, you can."

And it's true. You can absolutely manage your own investments throughout retirement. Just understand what you're signing up for.

If you are truly committed to investing for success in retirement, you must have significant time on your hands and a strong stomach to ensure you consistently execute upon your strategy. You can't let emotion be a factor, yet you may find that removing the emotional component is more difficult than you imagined.

What happens when the market experiences a sudden 20 percent drop? How comfortable are you in your allocation's ability to weather such volatility? Will you resist the urge to sell at a loss when push comes to shove?

No, you don't *need* to outsource your portfolio's investment management. However, when you choose to work with a wealth advisor, you give yourself the freedom of knowing your investments are being consistently monitored and adjusted as your life situation and market conditions evolve over time.

I'll use my firm, Falcon Wealth Advisors, as an example to illustrate my point that it often makes sense to outsource investment management to a wealth advisor.

- At Falcon Wealth Advisors, we start by developing a custom financial plan based on your personal financial situation, goals for the future, and any challenges you may face. We use this custom plan to guide all our decisions going forward, including your investment allocation.
- Once your plan is in place, our financial planners work with our team of investment analysts to develop a custom portfolio allocation precisely designed to navigate your challenges and achieve your long-term vision.
- From then on, our investment professionals diligently monitor your account for performance and opportunities, making changes as necessary along the way.

- Because minimizing your tax liabilities is a vital part of ensuring your success in retirement, our professionals are also looking for opportunities to implement strategic tax minimization strategies, such as tax-loss harvesting and asset location.

Cory, my business partner, didn't believe me when I asserted that I could figure out how to replace the engine in my car. I don't have a background in auto maintenance, but with enough time, effort, and YouTube videos, I'm pretty sure I could figure it out. Would I complete the task as well as a professional? Definitely not. Do I really want to spend so much time on this task? No way. Is it worth it to me to pay for the assistance and expertise of a trained professional? Absolutely.

Remember, your retirement isn't a car. It's your financial life. Could you cash out thirty-plus years of retirement savings to invest in an index fund or annuity? Yes, you could, but is that really the best strategy?

You only have one opportunity to invest for success in retirement. Consider enlisting the support, oversight, and experience of a wealth advisor to give you the best possible chance of achieving your goals.

TYPES OF INVESTMENT PRODUCTS

Let's just get this out of the way right up front. I despise investment products. I don't use them for myself, my family, or my clients. I believe they are a waste of money and not at all worth the fees investors must pay to access them.

Whew! I'm glad I got that off my chest. If you have the same opinion of investment products, feel free to skip ahead. If you're interested in learning about why I steer clear of these products, please read on.

MUTUAL FUNDS

You're likely familiar with mutual funds, but I'll provide a quick refresher.

Following are general characteristics of mutual funds.

- A mutual fund is a type of investment company that pools together investors' money and invests it according to a common theme or objective. For example, a mutual fund's objective may be to invest in North American technology-driven companies that have the potential for higher-than-normal growth.
- Investors can select a specific objective or strategy that meets their needs and access a diversified pool of stocks (or bonds if it's a bond fund) that are managed by an individual or team of professional investment managers.
- In exchange for managing your assets, the fund's investment manager charges an asset-based fee.
- You are collectively investing with thousands of other investors, which allows the investment manager to set low investment minimums. This makes mutual funds an easily accessible option for new investors and investors with few assets.
- Someone actively manages mutual funds, meaning the investment manager is actively buying and selling securities within the fund.
- A prospectus, which is a legal document that outlines the investment thesis and strategy, guides mutual funds.
- The prospectus includes the actual fees you pay, often buried deep in the document.
- The investment manager (or management team) focuses full time on the fund's strategy and is unaware of any individual investors or their needs/goals, financial situation, family, etc.
- Investors usually don't have access to speak to the fund's manager.

Here's the real kicker: mutual funds rarely outperform the market. In fact, research has shown that, over a twenty-year period ending December 2021, fewer than 10 percent of actively managed US stock funds beat their benchmarks.[14] And, the data isn't much better for short-term performance. According to the S&P Indices Versus Active (SPIVA) scorecard, 85.88 percent of fund managers underperformed the S&P over a three-year period (as of June 30, 2022).[15]

SPIVA US Scorecard
Mid-Year 2022
Report 1b: Percentage of US Equity Funds Underperforming Their Benchmarks (Based on Risk-Adjusted Return)

Fund Category	Comparison Index	3-Year (%)	5-Year (%)	10-Year (%)	15-Year (%)	20-Year (%)
All Domestic Funds	S&P Composite 1500	90.44	90.65	96.79	95.17	96.93
All Large-Cap Funds	S&P 500	87.06	88.71	96.81	92.48	96.89
All Mid-Cap Funds	S&P Mid-Cap 400	67.11	56.72	81.51	88.64	92.37
All Small-Cap Funds	S&P Small-Cap 600	80.83	74.91	90.99	91.05	93.69
All Multi-Cap Funds	S&P Composite 1500	90.15	88.26	96.08	94.08	95.74
Large-Cap Growth Funds	S&P 500 Growth	89.38	91.29	96.70	99.52	100.00
Large-Cap Core Funds	S&P 500	74.77	86.57	95.85	94.94	98.13

14   Jeff Sommer, "Actively Managed Mutual Funds Consistently Fail to Beat Markets, Study Finds," New York Times, December 2, 2022, https://www.nytimes.com/2022/12/02/business/stock-market-index-funds.html.

15   "SPIVA," S&P Dow Jones Indices, S&P Global, updated June 30, 2023, https://www.spglobal.com/spdji/en/research-insights/spiva.

Fund Category	Comparison Index	3-Year (%)	5-Year (%)	10-Year (%)	15-Year (%)	20-Year (%)
Large-Cap Value Funds	S&P 500 Value	65.53	71.25	86.71	72.09	83.10
Mid-Cap Growth Funds	S&P Mid-Cap 400 Growth	64.93	39.26	76.19	88.61	95.22
Mid-Cap Core Funds	S&P Mid-Cap 400	55.00	64.66	85.15	91.89	92.59
Mid-Cap Value Funds	S&P Mid-Cap 400 Value	53.13	68.52	75.00	88.17	82.69
Small-Cap Growth Funds	S&P Small-Cap 600 Growth	79.26	58.47	87.82	93.43	98.86
Small-Cap Core Funds	S&P Small-Cap 600	79.13	83.70	93.27	92.98	92.25
Small-Cap Value Funds	S&P Small-Cap 600 Value	80.85	82.27	91.16	91.66	94.15
Multi-Cap Growth Funds	S&P Composite 1500 Growth 84.80		88.36	94.17	98.31	97.75
Multi-Cap Core Funds	S&P Composite 1500	90.00	91.39	97.55	94.28	95.02
Multi-Cap Value Funds	S&P Composite 1500 Value	87.40	89.38	93.85	86.18	88.46
Real Estate Funds	S&P United States REIT	41.77	46.99	61.36	83.16	75.00

Source: "SPIVA," S&P Dow Jones Indices, S&P Global, updated June 30, 2023. Past performance is no guarantee of future results. https://www.spglobal.com/spdji/en/research-insights/spiva./.

So, if you invest in a mutual fund, you may be paying money to underperform a benchmark index.

Wait! It gets even worse.

What if you're working with a financial advisor who purchases mutual funds on your behalf?

If your current advisor invests your assets in mutual funds, you are likely paying an expense ratio to the fund and an additional asset-based fee to your advisor. If this is your fee arrangement, you essentially pay twice for the management of your assets.

For example, suppose you hire a financial advisor who charges a 1 percent fee on the assets he manages on your behalf. He then invests your assets in a variety of mutual funds with an average 1 percent expense ratio. You are now 2 percent in the hole before you even get started. Then, the funds you're invested in underperform their benchmarks by an average of 3 percent each year. That means you would need to achieve a 5 percent return just to break even with an unmanaged benchmark!

Wow! That strongly highlights why I despise mutual funds.

The only circumstance in which I, personally, would feel comfortable with a mutual fund is for an individual who manages his or her own portfolio and wishes to invest in something unique or niche, especially if this person has fewer assets and not much time to commit to research. In this situation, it's important to consider the following before selecting a mutual fund.

- **Track record**—Analyze at least five years of performance history to make sure the manager is adding value over time.
- **Turnover**—Review the management team to make sure there have been no key departures in the last few years. If the fund has new managers, the previous track record is no longer applicable. Look for a team that stays intact.
- **Fees**—How much does the fund charge to manage your assets? Is the expense worth it when compared to the performance the fund has historically delivered?
- **Investment philosophy**—Make sure the fund's philosophy and approach are in line with your overall goals.
- **Diversification**—Sometimes, mutual fund investors believe they are well diversified only to discover that their various funds have very similar holdings. It's important to achieve diversification among each fund's underlying holdings, as well as across various mutual funds.

After covering those mutual fund investment tips, I just need to say it one more time before I wrap up the topic. I am strongly opposed to including mutual funds in a portfolio managed by a professional advisor. If your current advisor uses mutual funds in your portfolio, it may be worth having a conversation about your net performance and fees.

EXCHANGE-TRADED FUNDS/INDEXED PRODUCTS

Exchange-traded funds (ETFs) and other indexed products are, typically, unmanaged funds. When you purchase an index fund, you're buying the whole market. For example, if you invest in an S&P 500 fund, you're buying into all 500 companies in the index. These are considered passive investments because no one is actively managing the holdings. Because there's no manager, the fees associated with these funds are typically very low.

Index funds often make the most sense for investors who are just getting started and want some market exposure. Maybe they're not yet at a point where it makes sense to hire a professional financial advisor (although, I always argue that it's best to start working with a wealth advisor as soon as possible). Index funds and ETFs can be a low-cost way to access the markets.

However, index funds have the same problem as mutual funds. If you're working with an advisor who invests your portfolio in an index fund, you're still being double charged for investment management. Why pay for investments that aren't even allocated with your best interest in mind?

At Falcon Wealth Advisors, we manage clients' portfolios in house using individual stocks and bonds, not investment products. More on that later, but I include that note here because I strongly believe it's wrong for an advisor to charge an asset-based management fee, then turn around and outsource the management of your assets to a mutual fund or index product.

VARIABLE ANNUITIES

In my opinion, variable annuities are the absolute worst of the worst. If you work with an "advisor" who tries to sell you an annuity, you should be careful to educate yourself on all of the specifics of the product being offered.

An annuity is a contract between an individual and a life insurance company in which the individual agrees to pay a certain amount of money (either as a lump sum payment or a series of payments over time) in return for a "guaranteed" stream of income in the future, typically throughout retirement. These types of arrangements can be structured in many different ways, and I could write an entire book just describing all the options, but I'll spare you the details.

In a nutshell, when you buy an annuity, you are paying for a "guarantee" that will return your assets to you in the form of regular income payments. However, that guarantee is only as good as the annuity's ability to pay it. There are no true guarantees for investing. In theory, however, the insurance company invests your assets and pays them out to you over time. Here's where things get dicey.

Fees

Annuities can be extremely profitable for the three parties involved in their operation (notice the investor is not included in this list):

1. **The insurance broker**—Annuities are most often sold by insurance brokers (sometimes, these brokers refer to themselves as

"advisors," but they are not to be confused with wealth advisors operating in a fiduciary capacity). The broker typically receives a commission-based fee on any annuity sold. Annuity commissions are high, and brokers have the potential to make a lot of money by selling these products. That's why the best, slickest sales people flock to annuity sales. It's an incredibly lucrative business to be in.

2. **The insurance company**—The insurance company underwriting the annuity makes money off these products in several ways.

    A. By collecting fees for account management and investing funds.

    B. By keeping a portion of the interest that your money earns while it is invested.

    C. By taking a profit once you annuitize your account and begin receiving payments.

3. **The underlying investment manager(s)**—When you purchase an annuity, the insurance company invests your assets on your behalf. If these assets are invested in a mutual fund or other fee-based investment product, you'll be charged investment management fees.

Security

The idea of having a guaranteed source of income that you can't outlive can be incredibly luring. You may not even mind paying an extreme premium for the peace of mind that comes with knowing your income needs will be met throughout retirement. Keep in mind, however, that the "guarantee" is only as strong as the insurance company.

What happens if the insurance company goes out of business? Your assets and future security could be completely wiped out.

Before investing in an annuity, ask yourself if that's a risk you're willing to take.

It's also important to remember that, to get your money out of an annuity, you must live long enough to recoup what you invested. And, if you're invested in a single life annuity, payments would stop after your death, leaving nothing for your spouse or heirs.

Complexity

Annuity products are incredibly complex. People purchase annuities without really understanding them because they're scared of outliving their assets, or they really liked the annuity sales person, only to regret the decision once it's too late. Annuity salespeople are great at capitalizing on investors' fear.

I can't even count the number of times I've counseled clients or prospects who were sold an annuity they didn't understand or didn't intend to buy. There's often a hefty fee associated with unwinding these products, which makes it difficult to undo the damage these predatory products can inflict on an investor's portfolio.

OTHER TYPES OF INVESTMENT PRODUCTS

Countless types of investment products are available, such as structured products, hedge funds, and other pooled vehicles, just to name a few. Many present the same challenges and drawbacks as the products detailed above. As long as you completely understand what you're getting into and it makes sense for your particular situation, there's nothing inherently wrong with investing in these products.

I advise you to be a fully informed consumer. If you're working

with an advisor who uses any type of investment product, it may be worth asking, "Why?" and inquiring about more cost-effective options.

IF NOT INVESTMENT PRODUCTS, THEN WHAT?

Now that I've utterly scared you away from investment products, you may wonder, *What's left to invest in?*

At Falcon Wealth Advisors, our clients don't have to worry about prospectuses, hidden fees, or complex investment structures. Why? Because we invest directly in stocks, bonds, and options, eliminating the middleman. Not only is this a more cost-effective approach (because our clients pay only one investment management fee), it also allows us to develop a truly customized portfolio based on each client's specific financial situation, goals, and challenges.

I'll provide additional details on our specific approach in just a bit, but I believe if you are supported by an experienced, knowledgeable wealth advisor, you shouldn't need to pay excessive fees for investment products that offer subpar performance and a generic investment allocation.

You deserve better.

HOW TO TURN YOUR RETIREMENT SAVINGS INTO MONTHLY INCOME

In this section, I cover several strategies that we at Falcon Wealth Advisors implement for our clients. Your wealth advisor should be able to determine the right mix of strategies based on your personal financial situation and retirement goals.

The first way we generate retirement income is through the purchase of interest-paying bonds. In contrast, when you purchase a stock, you are buying a stake of ownership in a company. When you purchase a bond, you are making a loan to a company, municipality, or government. In return, you are typically paid a regular interest rate. At the bond's maturity date, the borrower pays back your full principal amount, known as the bond's face value.

You can see how bond interest, when included as part of a diversified portfolio, can add to your monthly income stream. Another advantage to using bonds in your retirement investment portfolio is that they are typically less volatile than stocks. However, bonds don't offer the same growth opportunities as stocks, so it's important to determine an appropriate mix of both stocks and bonds that allows your portfolio to continue growing while also supporting your monthly income needs.

At Falcon Wealth Advisors, we typically consider three types of bonds for inclusion in our clients' portfolios.

1. **Municipal bonds**—Sometimes referred to as Munis, these bonds are issued by local, county, and state governments. They are commonly issued as a way to finance capital expenditures, such as the construction of bridges, schools, or highways. The main benefit to municipal bonds is that the interest paid is typically exempt from federal taxes, as well as state taxes if the investor lives in the issuer's state.

2. **Government bonds**—Government bonds are debt securities issued by a government (such as the US Treasury) to support spending and other obligations. Because they are backed by the full faith and credit of a government, they are typically considered risk-free when held to maturity. However, because

they are so safe, they generally pay lower interest rates than other types of bonds.

3. **Corporate bonds**—As the name suggests, corporations issue bonds to raise capital. These bonds are backed by the issuing company's ability to pay, which makes them riskier than municipal or government bonds. However, because they are riskier, they generally pay the highest interest rates of the three bond types. Corporate bonds range widely in quality and risk, so it's important to do your research before investing.

You may notice that I do not include high-yield/junk bonds or international bonds in my list. That's because I don't believe they're worth the additional risk. In my experience, there's plenty of income to be generated by high-quality, investment-grade corporate, government, and municipal bonds.

PREFERRED STOCK

When I think of preferred stocks, I think of them as a hybrid between bonds and common stock.

The following are similarities between preferred stocks and bonds:

- Both provide regular income to investors. Bonds pay interest and preferred stocks pay dividends.
- Preferred stock can be callable, meaning the issuing organization can eventually purchase preferred stock shares back by paying shareholders the current market value. This is like being paid a bond's face value at maturity or a bond being called in the same way.
- Preferred stock and bonds are both issued to raise capital.

Listed below are similarities between preferred stocks and common stocks:

• Like common stocks, preferred stocks are ownership in a company.
• Preferred stocks and common stocks both offer growth potential within a portfolio.

Because of these characteristics, preferred stocks are typically riskier than bonds and safer than stocks. Unlike common stocks, preferred stocks do not have voting rights. Also, the dividends on some types of preferred stock can become variable after a certain period.

Preferred stocks can be a great enhancement to an investor's retirement income, but it's important to understand that they reflect both the best and worst of stocks and bonds.

STOCK DIVIDENDS

Stocks typically fall into one of two categories:

1. Value (or income) stocks
2. Growth stocks

Certain market environments favor growth stocks, while other market environments favor value stocks, which is why it often makes sense to have an allocation to both. While growth stocks typically have more potential to (you guessed it!) grow over time, value stocks often have the benefit of issuing regular dividends, which can be a great source of retirement income.

Here's an example of how a dividend may work. Say you own 1,000 shares of a dividend-paying stock that's currently trading at

$100 per share. The value of your holding is $100,000 ($100 per share × 1,000 shares = $100,000). The stock issues a $1 per share dividend, and you receive $1,000 ($1 per share × 1,000 shares = $1,000). Following the dividend payment, the stock's value drops by an amount equal to the dividend paid, which means it is now worth $99 per share. You still own 1,000 shares of the stock, but that ownership is now valued at $99,000 rather than $100,000 ($99 per share × 1,000 shares = $99,000). So, you still have the same amount of net value as before, but you have an extra $1,000 you can use to support your lifestyle in retirement, without the need to sell any shares.

When analyzing potential value stocks to include in a client's portfolio, I typically look for companies that have a history of increasing their dividends over time, while also having the potential for future growth. When combined with growth stocks, value stocks can be a smart way to generate both growth and income within a portfolio.

OPTION PREMIUMS

At Falcon Wealth Advisors, we use options as an enhancement to an underlying security. Options allow the security holder to make a contract to buy or sell the security for a certain price during a predetermined time frame in the future. There are many types of options, and they can quickly become very complicated. Options can apply to a variety of security types. For this discussion, I'm going to focus on a conservative option strategy we at Falcon Wealth Advisors often apply to stocks—the covered call.

A covered call is an overlay strategy that can generate what some people consider a synthetic form of a dividend. As the owner of a stock, you can sell a covered call to someone else who agrees to pay for the right to acquire shares of your stock in the future,

on a predetermined date for a predetermined price. Basically, a covered call allows you to sell the potential upside of a stock to generate income.

I'll get into the specifics of options in Chapter Five. For now, I just wanted to mention that option premiums are another way to generate income. The caveat here is that these are complex strategies that only make sense for specific investors with specific stock holdings. They should only be attempted under the guidance of an experienced wealth advisor.

TRIMMING APPRECIATED STOCKS

If you have a growth stock that has appreciated in value, it may make sense to sell part of your position to fund your current lifestyle. This generally isn't the first strategy you should turn to because once you sell a position, it's gone, and you no longer have the potential for future growth or income on that security. However, under certain circumstances, it might make sense to trim back some of your appreciated holdings.

With all the strategies I mentioned in this section, the most important objective is to establish a monthly stream of income to support you throughout retirement. We can accomplish this in multiple ways, without the need to resort to expensive investment products, such as annuities and mutual funds. Just be sure to work with a wealth advisor who has the knowledge and experience necessary to develop a custom retirement income strategy that meets your specific needs and helps you live your desired lifestyle.

HOW TO AVOID RUNNING OUT OF MONEY IN RETIREMENT

Hands down, the number one question I get from clients planning for retirement is, "How can I make sure I won't run out of

money?" Even clients with millions of dollars at their fingertips lose sleep worrying that it won't be enough to last for the rest of their lives.

In this section, I share some simple tips to help ensure you have enough money to last throughout retirement, but you need a financial plan in place. Without a financial plan, you simply won't have the clarity you need to plan for a lifetime of monthly income.

Work with a wealth advisor. Implement a custom financial plan to meet your needs and achieve your goals. Update that plan regularly to keep up with your ever-evolving life. In my opinion, that's one of the best ways to ensure you won't run out of money in retirement.

The following tips should all be integrated as part of your financial planning process.

TIP #1—UNDERSTAND THE TRAJECTORY OF YOUR FINANCIAL PLAN

As part of the financial planning process, your advisor should model the trajectory of your retirement savings. Clients' various trajectories can vary widely based on their specific spending habits and retirement goals. For example:

- Client A's assets are projected to grow throughout retirement.
- Client B's assets are projected to remain consistent, neither growing nor shrinking during retirement.
- Client C's assets are projected to decrease over time throughout retirement.

It's not necessarily better to grow your assets throughout retirement, if that's not part of your plan. For example, perhaps Client C intends to give away his assets to loved ones and charities throughout his lifetime. Maybe he decides that his accounts only

need to last him until he's eighty-five, at which point, if he needs additional income, he'll sell his home and live off the proceeds.

Perhaps Client A has a special needs grandson she wishes to provide for and is working to grow her assets in a trust for his benefit.

Both are very personal retirement goals. The important thing here is to understand your financial plan's trajectory and ensure it helps you achieve your specific version of retirement success.

TIP #2—SPEND LESS THAN YOU MAKE

This one may seem obvious, but it may surprise you how many retirees don't have a firm grasp on how much they're spending compared to how much they're bringing in. This is something people often think about in their working years, but it can get overlooked in retirement. When you have a finite amount of assets that must last your entire life, it can be difficult to gauge how your spending is affecting that pool.

To avoid outliving your assets, it's essential to spend less than you bring in. This is especially true in an inflationary environment when your purchasing power is being depleted.

The first step is to understand the exact amount of income you bring in each month. Consider all sources, such as dividends, interest, pension payments, retirement plan distributions, Social Security, earnings from an encore career or part-time job, rental income, etc.

Once you've identified how much you bring in each month, start tracking your spending. Review all bank and investment statements for the last thirty to sixty days to understand how much goes out each month. Don't forget about less-frequent payments, such as insurance premiums, car registration fees, etc.

Then, compare the amount you spend to the amount you bring in each month. Is your level of spending sustainable over

the long term? If not, it may be time to find ways to either cut back or enhance your income stream (by taking on a part-time job, for example).

TIP #3—INVEST WISELY

I'll highlight specific investment types later in this section, but in any discussion about how to maintain assets throughout retirement, it's vital to address the importance of a proper asset allocation. You should have an appropriate allocation to both growth and value/income assets.

Growth investments help your portfolio keep up with inflation over time, while value/income assets can help cover your daily living expenses. If you are too heavily allocated to growth assets, you may be forced to sell out of investments at a loss to fund your lifestyle. If you're too heavily allocated to value/income investments, you may run out of purchasing power to support your future needs.

Once you have worked with your wealth advisor to establish an appropriate investment allocation, be sure to review your strategy regularly and make changes as necessary to keep up with your ever-evolving life and financial situation.

TIP #4—BE FLEXIBLE

I'll say it again—a financial plan is not a roadmap. It's not set in stone. It's important to review your financial plan regularly and make changes as necessary to help ensure it continues to meet your needs. Don't get so fixated on last year's strategy that you fail to update your plan to account for this year's situation. Be open to change and reevaluate your strategy as necessary to help ensure it continues to meet your needs.

TIP #5—ALIGN YOUR SPENDING WITH YOUR VALUES

Ask yourself, "What do I value?" "How do I want to spend my time?" "What are the most important things in my life?" Then, structure your spending accordingly.

At this point in the book, you already know that I love playing golf. It's my very favorite hobby, and when I'm retired, I plan to spend a lot of time on the golf course. I would gladly forgo many other expenses so I could focus my spending on playing golf.

Spending in retirement is about priorities. Understand what your priorities are and structure your spending habits accordingly. This will give you the best possible chance of both finding fulfillment and maintaining your assets to cover the expenses that matter most to you.

CHAPTER FIVE

Stocks and Bonds

STOCKS

As I mentioned earlier, a stock represents a piece of ownership in a company. When you purchase a stock, you purchase the opportunity to grow your portfolio alongside a company. The company uses your money to fuel that growth. The risk you take is that the value of the company could go down, which would make your stock shares worth less than when you purchased them. Keep in mind, however, that you don't lock in that loss until you sell the stock for less than you paid for it.

WHAT ROLE DO STOCKS PLAY IN A PORTFOLIO?

Stocks are intended to fuel a portfolio's growth. Many investment options offer growth opportunities, such as real estate, private businesses, etc. However, stocks offer a passive way to achieve portfolio growth, so you can focus your time on more important matters.

Keep in mind, however, that stocks are most effective when used as a long-term investment. You typically don't want to buy

stocks with any assets you plan to spend over the course of the next five to ten years. If you must access stock to fund your lifestyle, you may end up selling when the market is down, thereby locking in a loss. For someone living in retirement, this type of loss can do permanent damage to a portfolio.

If you're investing in the stock market, make sure your objective is to grow your money, without touching it for the next five to ten years and beyond.

WAYS TO BUY STOCKS

There are two main ways to purchase stocks:

1. Directly from an exchange or platform
2. Through an investment product

I bet you can guess which method I prefer.

At Falcon Wealth Advisors, we never use investment products because we have witnessed the harm high fees can have on investors' long-term investment returns.

We only manage individual stock portfolios for our clients. Not only does this typically result in lower fees, it also gives us control and the ability to ensure each and every holding is in line with a client's financial plan, current situation, and goals for the future.

THE IMPORTANCE OF BEING DIVERSIFIED

When investing in a stock portfolio, you don't want to put all your eggs in one basket. If you go all in on one company, and that company's stock tanks in value, you could be in trouble. On the flip side, there are no benefits to being overly diversified.

If the mutual fund way of thinking has influenced you, then you might believe you need hundreds of stocks to achieve diversification. However, it's been illustrated time and again that you can achieve diversification with twenty-five to thirty-five stock holdings. At that point, investment risk levels off. Investing in more than thirty-five stocks does not reduce portfolio risk.

Strategy Implementation

How much risk can be diversified away?

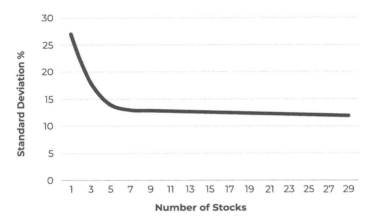

Average risk (standard deviation) of portfolios containing different numbers of stocks. The stocks were selected randomly from stocks traded on the New York Exchange from 2002 through 2007. Notice that diversification reduces risk rapidly at first, then more slowly.

Source: Brealey, Myers and Allen, *Principles of Corporate Finance*, New York: McGraw-Hill Irwin, (2011).

While it's not possible to fully diversify risk away, maintaining diversification is important. A portfolio that is properly diversified will have some stocks that are performing well and others that are performing poorly. However, that's not a bad thing. As market conditions shift over time, the stocks performing poorly can quickly replace the others as top performers.

Callan publishes a great resource called "The Callan Periodic Table of Investment Returns," which perfectly illustrates my point. In the following table, look at large-cap equity as an example. In 2022, four asset classes outperformed large-cap equities, which experienced a −18.11 percent return for the year. However, just one year prior, in 2021, large-cap equities outperformed all other asset classes, with a 28.71 percent return.

THE CALLAN PERIODIC TABLE OF INVESTMENT RETURNS
*Annual Returns for Key Indices Ranked in
Order of Performance (2004–2023)*

2004	2005	2006	2007	2008
Real Estate 37.96%	Emerging Market Equity 34.00%	Real Estate 42.12%	Emerging Market Equity 39.38%	US Fixed Income 5.24%
Emerging Market Equity 25.55%	Real Estate 15.35%	Emerging Market Equity 32.17%	Developed Ex-US Equity 12.44%	Global Ex-US Fixed 4.39%
Developed Ex-US Equity 20.38%	Developed Ex-US Equity 14.47%	Developed Ex-US Equity 25.71%	Global Ex-US Fixed 11.03%	Cash Equivalent 2.06%
Small-Cap Equity 18.33%	Large-Cap Equity 4.91%	Small-Cap Equity 18.37%	US Fixed Income 6.97%	High Yield −26.16%
Global Ex-US Fixed 12.54%	Small-Cap Equity 4.55%	Large-Cap Equity 15.79%	Large-Cap Equity 5.49%	Small-Cap Equity −33.79%
High Yield 11.13%	Cash Equivalent 3.07%	High Yield 11.85%	Cash Equivalent 5.00%	Large-Cap Equity −37.00%
Large-Cap Equity 10.88%	High Yield 2.74%	Global Ex-US Fixed 8.16%	High Yield 1.87%	Developed Ex-US Equity −43.56%
US Fixed Income 4.34%	US Fixed Income 2.43%	Cash Equivalent 4.85%	Small-Cap Equity −1.57%	Real Estate −48.21%
Cash Equivalent 1.33%	Global Ex-US Fixed −8.65%	US Fixed Income 4.33%	Real Estate −7.39%	Emerging Market Equity −53.33%

2009	2010	2011	2012	2013
Emerging Market Equity 78.51%	Small-Cap Equity 26.85%	US Fixed Income 7.84%	Real Estate 27.73	Small-Cap Equity 38.82
High Yield 58.21%	Real Estate 19.63%	High Yield 4.98%	Emerging Market Equity 18.23%	Large-Cap Equity 32.39%
Real Estate 37.13%	Emerging Market Equity 18.88%	Global Ex-US Fixed 4.36%	Developed Ex-US Equity 16.41%	Developed Ex-US Equity 21.02%
Developed Ex-US Equity 33.67%	High Yield 15.12%	Large-Cap Equity 2.11%	Small-Cap Equity 16.35%	High Yield 7.44%
Small-Cap Equity 27.17%	Large-Cap Equity 15.06%	Cash Equivalent 0.10%	Large-Cap Equity 16.00%	Real Estate 3.67%
Large-Cap Equity 26.47%	Developed Ex-US Equity 8.95%	Small-Cap Equity −4.18%	High Yield 15.81%	Cash Equivalent 0.07%
Global Ex-US Fixed 7.53%	US Fixed Income 6.54%	Real Estate −6.46%	US Fixed Income 4.21%	US Fixed Income −2.02%

2014	2015	2016	2017	2018
Real Estate 15.02%	Large-Cap Equity 1.38%	Small-Cap Equity 21.31%	Emerging Market Equity 37.28%	Cash Equivalent 1.87%
Large-Cap Equity 13.69%	US Fixed Income 0.55%	High Yield 17.13%	Developed Ex-US Equity 24.21%	US Fixed Income 0.01%
US Fixed Income 5.97%	Cash Equivalent 0.05%	Large-Cap Equity 11.96%	Large-Cap Equity 21.83%	High Yield −2.08%
Small-Cap Equity 4.89%	Real Estate −0.79%	Emerging Market Equity 11.19%	Small-Cap Equity 14.65%	Global Ex-US Fixed −2.15%
High Yield 2.45%	Developed Ex-US Equity −3.04%	Real Estate 4.06%	Global Ex-US Fixed 10.51%	Large-Cap Equity −4.38%
Cash Equivalent 0.03%	Small-Cap Equity −4.41%	Developed Ex-US Equity 2.75%	Real Estate 10.36%	Real Estate −5.63%
Emerging Market Equity −2.19%	High Yield −4.47%	US Fixed Income 2.65%	High Yield 7.50%	Small-Cap Equity −11.01%
Global Ex-US Fixed −3.09%	Global Ex-US Fixed −6.02%	Global Ex-US Fixed 1.49%	US Fixed Income 3.54%	Developed Ex-US Equity −14.09%
Developed Ex-US Equity −4.32%	Emerging Market Equity −14.92%	Cash Equivalent 0.33%	Cash Equivalent 0.86%	Emerging Market Equity −14.57%

2019	2020	2021	2022	2023
Large-Cap Equity	Small-Cap Equity	Large-Cap Equity	Cash Equivalent	Large-Cap Equity
31.49%	19.96%	28.71%	1.46%	26.29%
Small-Cap Equity	Large-Cap Equity	Real Estate	High Yield	Developed Ex-US Equity
25.52%	18.40	26.09%	−11.19%	17.94%
Developed Ex-US Equity	Emerging Market Equity	Small-Cap Equity	US Fixed Income	Small-Cap Equity
22.49%	18.31%	14.82%	−13.01%	16.93%
Real Estate	Global Ex-US Fixed	Developed Ex-US Equity	Developed Ex-US Equity	High Yield
21.91%	10.11%	12.62%	−14.29%	13.44%
Emerging Market Equity	Developed Ex-US Equity	High Yield	Large-Cap Equity	Emerging Market Equity
18.44%	7.59%	5.28%	−18.11%	9.83%
High Yield	US Fixed Income	Cash Equivalent	Global Ex-US Fixed	Real Estate
14.32%	7.51%	0.05%	−18.70%	9.67%
US Fixed Income	High Yield	US Fixed Income	Emerging Market Equity	Global Ex-US Fixed
8.72%	7.11%	−1.54%	−20.09%	5.72%
Global Ex-US Fixed	Cash Equivalent	Emerging Market Equity	Small-Cap Equity	US Fixed Income
5.09%	0.67%	−2.54%	−20.44%	5.53%
Cash Equivalent	Real Estate	Global Ex-US Fixed	Real Estate	Cash Equivalent
2.28%	−9.04%	−7.05%	−25.10%	5.01%

Source: Jay Kloepfer, "The Callan Periodic Table of Investment Returns: Year-End 2022," Callan Institute, accessed January 13, 2024, https://www.callan.com/research/2022-classic-periodic-table/#. A printable copy of The Callan Periodic Table of Investment Returns is available on our website at callan.com/periodic-table/. © 2024 Callan LLC. See "Disclosures" for full disclaimer.

Callan's Periodic Table of Investment Returns depicts annual returns for asset classes and cash equivalents, ranked from best to worst performance for each calendar year. The asset classes are color-coded to enable easy tracking over time. We describe the well-known, industry-standard market indices that we use as proxies for each asset class below.

Large Cap Equity (S&P 500) measures the performance of large capitalization US stocks. The S&P 500 is a market-value weighted index of 500 stocks. The weightings make each company's influence on the Index performance directly proportional to that company's market value.

Small Cap Equity (Russell 2000) measures the performance of small capitalization US stocks. The Russell 2000 is a market-value-weighted index of the 2,000 smallest stocks in the broad-market Russell 3000 Index.

Developed ex-US Equity (MSCI World ex-USA) is an index that is designed to measure the performance of Large- and Mid-Cap equities in developed markets in Europe, the Middle East, the Pacific region, and Canada.

Emerging Market Equity (MSCI Emerging Markets) is an index that is designed to measure the performance of equity markets in twenty-four emerging countries around the world.

US Fixed Income (Bloomberg US Aggregate Bond Index) includes US government, corporate, and mortgage-backed securities with maturities of at least one year.

High Yield (Bloomberg High Yield Bond Index) measures the market of USD-denominated, non-investment grade, fixed rate, taxable corporate bonds. Securities are classified as high yield if the middle rating of Moody's, Fitch, and S&P is Ba1/BB+/BB+ or below, excluding emerging market debt.

Global ex-US Fixed Income (Bloomberg Global Aggregate ex-US Bond Index) is an unmanaged index that is comprised of

several other Bloomberg indices that measure the fixed income performance of regions around the world, excluding the US.

Real Estate (FTSE EPRA Nareit Developed REIT Index) is designed to measure the stock performance of companies engaged in specific real estate activities in the North American, European, and Asian real estate markets.

Cash Equivalent (ninety-day T-bill) is a short-term debt obligation backed by the Treasury Department of the US government.

The Callan Periodic Table of Investment Returns conveys the strong case for diversification across asset classes (stocks versus bonds), capitalizations (large versus small), and equity markets (US versus global ex-US). The table highlights the uncertainty inherent in all capital markets. Rankings change every year. Also noteworthy is the difference between absolute and relative performance, as returns for the top-performing asset class span a wide range over the past twenty years.

Seeing the success of large-cap equities in 2021, what if you had sold your other investments and put everything you had into various large-cap equity stocks? Once 2022 hit, you'd probably deeply regret your decision.

A diversified portfolio that contains multiple asset classes will typically contain some investments that are performing well and others that are performing poorly. The same is true of a stock portfolio. If you are truly diversified, you can expect to have both winners and losers at any given point in time. What none of us can predict is the future. Today's losers may well be tomorrow's winners, and vice versa. That is why diversification is important.

When we evaluate stocks to include in a client's diversified portfolio, we typically conduct two types of analysis:

1. **Fundamental analysis**—A method of determining whether a stock is overvalued or undervalued based on underlying

economic conditions and the financial stability of the company. Considerations include earnings, cash flow, leadership team, etc.

2. **Technical analysis**—Considers patterns in the price of an investment to help predict the future direction of that investment's price. Has the stock been trending up or down? Is it due for a recovery or crash?

Generally, when investors see a stock price dropping, their natural reaction is to sell out. This is the exact opposite reaction you should have. By selling out, not only are you locking in losses, you are missing out on an opportunity to buy additional shares at a "discounted" price. As long as the stock's fundamentals remain strong, it may be wise to buy more of it. Conversely, if a stock continues going up in price, it likely makes sense to sell out of it, or at least trim it, and realize a profit.

In summary, if we could predict the future, we'd all be big winners in the stock market game. Unfortunately, none of us knows what's going to happen. Diversification can help smooth out a portfolio's returns both to the upside and the downside. When you have a diversified portfolio, you don't need to predict the future because you'll be well positioned for whatever comes your way.

MANAGING A CONCENTRATED STOCK POSITION

All that talk about diversification leads to a common challenge faced by many corporate associates—a heavy concentration in company stock.

Corporate associates often receive a portion of their compensation as company stock. This makes sense, as it aligns the incentives of corporate leaders with the success of the business.

As the company does well, associates benefit from a rising stock price. Over time, it's not uncommon for an employee's net worth to be heavily weighted in company stock.

As you near retirement, however, it's important to unwind some of this stock ownership to get back to the diversification we discussed earlier. There are challenges, pitfalls, and tax implications to selling off company stock positions, so it's important to work with a wealth advisor to implement strategies that make sense for your personal financial situation.

BONDS

Unlike stocks, which represent an ownership stake of a company, bonds are a loan to a company, government, municipality, etc. In exchange for receiving capital as a loan, the borrower agrees to pay you a certain interest rate over the course of the bond's term. Once the bond reaches a predetermined maturity date, the borrower pays back your principal, known as the bond's face value.

As I mentioned earlier, at Falcon Wealth Advisors, we typically consider three types of bonds for inclusion in our clients' portfolios.

1. Corporate Bonds
2. Government Bonds
3. Municipal Bonds

WHY USE BONDS?

Investment-grade bonds are generally less risky than stocks and can help smooth out market volatility. They also generally pay out regular interest payments that can enhance retirees' monthly income.

At Falcon Wealth Advisors, most of our clients are high-net-worth individuals. They have spent their careers building their wealth and they do not want to risk their portfolios in the hopes of doubling their assets. Instead, they want to protect their savings, grow their capital, and achieve a steady cash flow.

Bonds have the potential to counterbalance stock market risk, provide regular income to fund your retirement lifestyle, and protect the wealth you have worked so hard to build. That's why we include them in our clients' portfolios.

What Is a Bond Ladder?

A bond ladder is a strategy for managing the maturity dates of a bond portfolio. In a laddering strategy, investors evenly space the maturity dates of various bonds across a specific time frame. This allows for the reinvestment of the bonds' proceeds at regular intervals as they mature over time. This strategy can help minimize interest-rate risk, diversify credit risk, reduce reinvestment risk, and increase liquidity within the bond portfolio.

The following is an example of how a laddered bond portfolio works.

- Jane Investor, along with her wealth advisor, determines that she would benefit from investing $500,000 in a bond portfolio, using a five-year laddering strategy.
- With Jane's $500,000, the advisor purchases a $100,000 bond that matures in one year, a $100,000 bond that matures in two years, a $100,000 bond that matures in three years, a $100,000 bond that matures in four years and a $100,000 bond that matures in five years.
- Each $100,000 bond has a different maturity date and pays a different rate of interest.

- As each bond matures, the borrower repays Jane the bond's face value. The advisor uses the proceeds to purchase a new bond with an extended maturity date.
- Jane has a constant stream of regular interest payments from the various bonds that she uses to help fund her lifestyle in retirement.
- As interest rates rise, Jane can reinvest the proceeds of previous bonds into new bonds that are paying higher interest rates.
- As interest rates decrease, Jane continues to receive higher rates from the bonds she purchased when rates were higher.

When implemented correctly as part of a diversified investment management strategy, bond ladders can be a great way to generate income and protect an investor's short-term assets.

At Falcon Wealth Advisors we will shorten or extend the length of the bond ladder depending on the individual client's goals, interest rate environment, and overall financial plan.

Bond Risks

While bonds play an important role in any diversified investment portfolio, they are not without risk.

1. **Interest rate risk**—The risk that a bond's value will fall in the secondary market because there is more competition from newer bonds that pay higher interest rates. As interest rates move higher, bond prices decrease. You can avoid this risk by holding a bond until its maturity. If you are forced to sell prior to a bond's maturity, you may be subject to interest rate risk.
2. **Reinvestment risk**—This is the risk that, once a bond matures, its premium can only purchase a lower-rate bond than the one it is replacing. For example, say you own a ten-year bond

ladder during a period of declining interest rates. You hold a bond paying a 6 percent interest rate that is set to expire. Your only choice is to reinvest your premium payment in a bond paying 3 percent interest. While it's impossible to completely eliminate reinvestment risk, a bond ladder can help spread this risk out over several years, which is a benefit over having all your bonds mature at one time when interest rates are low.

3. **Default risk**—The risk that the bond issuer (borrower) is not able to meet its financial obligations, causing the bond to default. This risk is much more prevalent in certain high-yield bonds (aka "junk" bonds). There are multiple bond rating agencies that strive to help investors avoid the risk of default by issuing scores for various bonds. It's important to understand that if a bond is paying abnormally high interest rates, it likely has a higher level of default risk.

4. **Inflation risk**—The risk that inflation will erode the value of a fixed-price bond. For example, if you purchase a $10,000 bond that matures in ten years, you'll receive $10,000 when the bond matures. If inflation has been high during those ten years, your $10,000 will not have as much purchasing power as it did when you purchased the bond. The upside is that you likely received interest payments over the ten years you held the bond. However, inflation risk again highlights the importance of having a portion of your portfolio invested in growth assets, such as stocks, to keep up with inflation.

OPTIONS

Before we get started on options, I'd like to remind my readers that neither this section, nor any other part of this book, is intended as investment advice. Options can be a great way to potentially enhance a portfolio's returns in specific situations, but

they do not make sense for everyone. Also, if an option contract is improperly executed, an investor can stand to lose thousands (if not tens or hundreds of thousands) of dollars.

So, please read this section as background information to help you understand how options contracts can potentially enhance a portfolio's returns. Then, consult with a wealth advisor to determine whether options make sense for your personal financial situation and retirement strategy.

WHAT ARE OPTIONS?

Options are derivative contracts that trade through the Chicago Board of Options Exchange. They are basically a type of security placed as an overlay on an underlying security. They function as contracts that are set to execute during an agreed-upon timeframe at an agreed-upon price.

An option's value is based on time, price, and the volatility of an underlying security. Options can be placed on a wide variety of securities; however, for the sake of this discussion, I'm going to refer only to stocks.

Option contracts trade in blocks of 100 shares. For this reason, options strategies typically only make sense for investors who hold several thousand shares, as an investor with only a few hundred shares probably won't reap much benefit.

HOW DO OPTIONS WORK?

Option contracts can function in many ways, quickly becoming extremely complex. At Falcon Wealth Advisors, we believe the most viable option strategy for our clients is the covered call. That's what I'm going to highlight here. The following example illustrates how covered call writing works.

- Joe Investor owns 100 shares of XYZ Stock, which has a current market value of $40 per share.
- Joe and his wealth advisor decide to sell one covered call option for XYZ Stock in April at $45. (Remember that one covered call option equals 100 shares.)
- For writing the covered call, Joe receives a premium of $1 per share, for a total of $100.
- Joe then waits for April to see if the stock price will hit $45 per share and trigger his sale.

There are two possible outcomes to Joe's option strategy.

1. XYZ Stock hits $45.01 and the option exercises. Joe's shares are automatically sold, and he receives the predetermined sales price of $45 per share. (Note that if the value of XYZ Stock bounces to $100 per share, or any other value greater than $45, Joe still receives $45.)
2. XYZ Stock never reaches $45 during the designated timeframe. The option expires and Joe retains ownership of his shares.

Regardless of whether the options contract is executed, Joe retains his $100 premium.

Strategy Implementation

Covered Call Writing

Own 100 Shares of XYZ Stock @ $40	Possible Outcomes

• Sell 1 Covered Call Option for April XYZ Stock @ $45
• Premium of $1.00/per share
  ◦ Collect $100
• Wait During Time Period
	• XYZ Stock @ $45.01 and/or Above
	  ◦ Option Exercises
	    ▪ Sell XYZ Stock @ $45
	• XYZ Stock @ $45.00 and Below
	  ◦ Option Expires
	    ▪ You Retain XYZ Stock
	• You Keep Premium Regardless

1 Covered Call Option = 100 Shares

For Illustration Purposes Only

WHAT IS THE IDEAL MARKET FOR OPTIONS?

When it comes to selling options, the more market volatility, the better. Volatile markets yield higher premiums. When the market goes up, everyone is happy. When markets are flat or trending down, options can offer an opportunity to enhance an investor's returns.

WHO WOULD WANT TO BUY A COVERED CALL?

Sometimes, a client will ask, "Who's purchasing these options contracts?" In other words, who would agree to purchase shares at a higher price in the future when they can just buy them today for a lower cost? This is a great question.

Typically, those on Wall Street who purchase these contracts are highly speculative investors. Using the example above, these investors are betting they can purchase your shares for $45 and then turn around and sell them for $100. For the opportunity to

do so, they only have to pay a $100 premium, not the full stock value.

Besides speculative investors, large institutions sometimes use option contracts as a hedge to cover their positions.

Whatever the reason for purchasing a call strategy, the only way to make money is for the underlying investment to increase in value. That's a risk we would never take in our clients' portfolios, but on the sell side, it can be a good strategy to generate additional retirement income.

A FINAL NOTE

You should not try this on your own! Trading options is a highly complex strategy that can quickly go south if you make an incorrect decision or a mistake when you set your contract. Only attempt an options strategy under the guidance of an experienced wealth advisor.

CHAPTER SIX

What to Look for in an Advisor

Feeling a little overwhelmed by all the information I've thrown your way? I know it's a lot to take in, and you may wonder if you'll need to spend the bulk of your retirement just looking after your investments and financial plan. The good news is, there are many qualified wealth advisors out there who will gladly take on the heavy lifting so you can live life with confidence.

The question now becomes, "What should I look for in a wealth advisor?" In other words, "How can I make sure the advisor I choose will do a good job for my family and me?" Choosing the right wealth advisor for your particular situation can be a tough decision, which is why I've dedicated this entire chapter to helping you navigate this important topic.

The following are five important characteristics to look for when evaluating potential wealth advisors.

#1—AN ADVISOR WHO IS HELD TO A FIDUCIARY STANDARD

The financial services industry allows advisors to serve in different capacities, depending on the role they fulfill. The challenge is, many advisors use the same job titles, so it can be difficult to know at a glance who you're working with.

Before choosing an advisor, understand what capacity each potential candidate serves in and where his or her loyalties lie. There are three main types of advisors.

INSURANCE AGENTS AND BROKERS

Don't let insurance agents and investment brokers who are labeled as "financial advisors" deceive you. These professionals are salespeople whose main goal is to sell you an insurance or investment product. Similar to other salespeople, agents and brokers are paid a commission based on sales, which means their financial incentives may be in direct conflict with yours.

These types of advisors are held to a "suitability standard" by the Financial Industry Regulatory Authority (FINRA). This standard requires that the advisor "must have a reasonable basis to believe that a recommended transaction or investment strategy involving a security or securities is *suitable* for the customer." The suitability standard only requires that an investment is suitable to the client's current circumstances, but the agent or broker is free to recommend products with high commissions that put more money in his/her pocket.

ADVISORS SERVING AS FIDUCIARIES

In contrast to insurance agents and brokers, advisors serving as fiduciaries adhere to a (you guessed it!) fiduciary standard, which means these advisors have a legal, ongoing obligation to

put clients' interests ahead of their own, at all times and in all situations.

Instead of charging commissions based on product sales, these advisors are typically "fee-only," which means they charge a percentage fee based on the assets under their management. This helps align the advisor's interests with those of the client because the advisor's fee grows in proportion with the client's portfolio. It also removes the need to generate product sales or generate frequent transactions within a client's portfolio.

Advisors serving in a fiduciary capacity may also charge a flat fee, either hourly, project-based, retainer-based, etc. The key here is that advisors serving as fiduciaries do not receive added compensation based on the products they sell or transactions they initiate. Their compensation is aligned with the client's best interests.

DUALLY REGISTERED ADVISORS

To complicate matters, certain financial advisors serve as agents or brokers in some situations and as fiduciaries in others. This means the standard to which the advisor is held (suitability versus fiduciary) changes as he or she alternates between the two roles. Because of this constant shift in roles, it can be difficult to know what "hat" the advisor is wearing at any given time.

While on the surface, the difference between the suitability and fiduciary standards may seem insignificant, in practice, it can mean the difference between achieving your long-term financial goals or not. Agents and brokers are focused on the transaction and are financially incentivized to recommend products with higher fees, which can drastically erode your savings and investment returns over time.

In contrast, advisors serving as fiduciaries are focused on building long-term relationships with clients because their success is

directly related to the success of their clients. Because the advisor is paid a fee that is independent of product sales or transaction frequency, he or she is in a better position to serve clients' best interests.

When you're interviewing potential advisors, one of the first questions I recommend you ask is, "Are you held to a fiduciary standard of care?" The answer should be a simple, "Yes." Any other answer may indicate that the advisor's loyalties lie elsewhere.

Now, before we move on, I want to clarify that advisors who are held to a suitability standard are in no way bad or evil. They serve a purpose in the industry just as advisors who serve as fiduciaries serve a purpose. However, it's important to understand what that purpose is and to set your expectations accordingly.

For example, when you go to a car dealership to buy a new car, you know that the salesperson is there to make money off of you. You would never expect the salesperson to recommend a cheaper car than the one you're interested in. Instead, you prepare yourself for the sale. You know you're going to be encouraged to upgrade your car's features and purchase multiple extended warranties, thereby increasing your purchase price, and ultimately the salesperson's commission.

The key here is that you enter the relationship understanding that your interests are not aligned with the salesperson's interests, and that's okay because you need to buy a car. The same is true when working with an agent or broker. The important thing is to understand the role the "advisor" is serving in and to set your expectations accordingly.

If your expectation is to work with an advisor who will provide ongoing advice focused on helping you achieve your personal financial goals, make sure you're working with an advisor serving as a fiduciary.

#2—STANDARDIZED SERVICE/CUSTOM ADVICE

When interviewing an advisor, it's important to ask about his or her service model. Choose an advisor who has a set standard of service and can provide a consistent client experience. Why is this important? Because you need to know what services and support you can expect to receive. By working with an advisor who has a set process in place, you can also be more confident that nothing important will fall through the cracks.

In my experience, advisors who lack a consistent service model raise two red flags.

1. **They may not have many clients**—There's just no way to effectively serve a large group of clients when you must do things differently every time. While you want to choose an advisor with a manageable workload, choosing one with too few clients may mean he or she lacks experience.

2. **They may be disorganized**—You may have a hard time knowing what to expect from one interaction to the next due to their disorganization. It also means important matters may be overlooked.

Your advisor should articulate a clear service model and process that is implemented across the entire firm. This means that, even if your particular contact is out of the office, another team member can step in and provide the same level of exceptional service.

Another benefit to having a standardized service model is that it provides the advisor with the freedom and flexibility to offer truly custom advice. When an advisor is supported by an established process, he or she no longer needs to worry about daily administrative tasks and can focus instead on getting to

know you and implementing custom strategies to help solve your particular challenges.

#3—CLEAR AND TRANSPARENT FEES

Outside of the financial services industry, it's uncomplicated what we're paying for goods and services and what we can expect to receive in return. When shopping for a new toaster, for example, we can easily compare one toaster's features to another and decide which one to purchase based on the cost, functionality, and value provided. We can shop around to make sure we're getting the best deal and make an apples-to-apples comparison of various toasters' brand, quality, price, etc.

Within the financial industry, however, fees are often buried deep in bulky prospectuses and woven into complex investment products. To add even more complexity, professionals can structure their compensation in different ways.

I'm going to make things simple for you…

- If an advisor can't look you in the eye and tell you the exact amount you will pay for his/her services, turn and run!
- If an advisor tells you something is "free," run!
- If an advisor is at all secretive about fees, run!
- If the cost structure is any more complicated to understand than the amount you're paying for a toaster, run!

An advisor's fees should be presented in a clear and transparent manner. You have a right to know exactly what you're paying, how and when you will be billed, and exactly what you're receiving in return. Period.

At Falcon Wealth Advisors, we post our costs on our website.

We also provide quarterly statements that detail exactly what costs each client paid during that period. We discuss our costs freely and openly at every client review meeting. Because we don't use investment products, our clients never pay expense ratios, revenue sharing, or other product-based fees.

Before choosing an advisor, make sure you know what you're paying and exactly what you're receiving in return.

#4—EXPERIENCE WORKING WITH OTHERS IN SIMILAR SITUATIONS

Another important consideration when interviewing an advisor is whether he or she has experience working with clients with similar financial goals as yours.

For example, corporate executives often have concentrated stock positions and various stock options that an advisor will need to help navigate. Small business owners may be interested in finding an advisor who has experience managing the complexities of a business sale. Doctors who own their own practice may need additional guidance regarding what type of insurance they need for both themselves and their practice.

An advisor who has experience navigating the specific challenges you face can provide you with additional insight and the confidence that you have a trusted partner who truly understands your situation. Your advisor should clearly articulate his or her niche market and offer specific details about his/her experience working with clients facing similar challenges.

Our specific expertise revolves around all aspects of retirement planning. Our experience and credentials make us uniquely qualified to help clients navigate decisions related to required minimum distributions (RMDs), Social Security, Medicare, Roth conversions, retirement income planning, portfolio management,

etc. Because we deal with retirement planning complexities on a regular basis, clients seeking these services can be confident that we have the experience to help them.

We also have expertise helping high-income earners navigate issues such as where to save and how, tax-efficient investing and withdrawal strategies, early retirement, net worth diversification, and more.

Whatever your specific situation and challenges may be, it's important to find an advisor who has experience navigating them.

#5—A WILLINGNESS TO COLLABORATE WITH OTHER FINANCIAL PROFESSIONALS

No single advisor can be all things to all clients. Your financial life is complex, and you need a team of experienced professionals who are willing to work together on your behalf. Based on your specific needs, these professionals may include any combination of the following.

- Wealth advisor
- Certified public accountant (CPA)
- Estate planning attorney
- Insurance agent
- Mortgage broker
- Real estate agent

Because your wealth advisor is responsible for managing your overall financial health, he or she should be willing to work with other professionals and serve as the "quarterback" of your various relationships. It's important that your advisor be comfortable pro-actively communicating with your other professionals to ensure that all aspects of your financial life are integrated into your financial plan and working together to achieve your goals.

An experienced advisor will also have trusted relationships with multiple professionals that he or she can refer you to if you require additional services, if necessary. (Just make sure your advisor never receives referral fees or other kickbacks for doing so.)

QUESTIONS TO ASK A POTENTIAL ADVISOR

It may be helpful to compile a list of questions to ask potential financial advisors. Consider the following as a starting point.

- Are you held to a fiduciary standard of care?
- For how many years have you been serving as a wealth advisor?
- How are you compensated? Exactly what fees do you charge? How and when do you charge these fees?
- Do you use outside investment products? If so, are there additional management fees, expense ratios, revenue sharing agreements, or any other fees that would increase the amount I pay?
- What is your service model? What services, exactly, will you provide to me?
- What designations do you and your team members carry?
- What are your specific areas of expertise?
- What is your niche market?
- Will you serve as my primary contact, or will I be working with someone else?
- Do you operate independently of all investment managers, brokerages, insurance agents, etc.? If not, how do you avoid potential conflicts of interest?
- Are you supported by a team of professionals? If so, how many and in what roles do they serve?
- Do you work with a qualified custodian to hold client assets?

- Are you open to working with outside professionals such as CPAs, estate planning attorneys, etc.?
- How quickly do you respond to client calls and emails? Do you have a firm-wide service standard for getting back to clients?

One last tip before I wrap up this chapter. Remember that whoever you choose as your advisor will play an important role in your life and the lives of your loved ones. You should feel comfortable discussing your most personal financial goals and life dreams with your advisor. You should also be able to picture yourself calling that person for help when life throws unexpected curveballs your way.

It's also important to work with an advisor who values education as part of the planning process and will take time to explain every action he or she is taking on your behalf. It's your financial life, after all. You have a right to be fully aware of and confident in all strategies employed on your behalf.

If you can't envision yourself building a trusted, long-term relationship with the person sitting across the desk from you, keep looking. The right advisor is out there. Don't settle for anyone you don't feel completely comfortable working with.

Conclusion

Congratulations! You have taken the time to enhance your financial literacy and open the doorway to learning more about what your financial plan means to you. I want to confirm that having emotions, concerns, and fears are all normal and okay when it comes to planning for your retirement. Now you are better equipped to handle and hopefully avoid some common mistakes.

You have learned about how to find your purpose and how to check in with yourself to truly define what the next phase of your life might look like. You have learned about the core concepts of having a financial plan and what it means to truly understand where you're headed. We have discussed major concerns with health insurance and social security. We have also addressed investment products and why I believe firmly in not double paying for investment management. I have addressed common themes when looking to hire a wealth advisor. At my firm we feel our responsiveness, in house collaborative team approach, and transparent investment strategy are a few things that sets us apart.

There's no denying it—planning for retirement can be a daunting, overwhelming task. When you're thinking about planning

for the next several decades of your life, there's a lot at stake. Fortunately, with focused financial planning, custom strategies, and smart goal setting, you can successfully achieve the retirement of your dreams.

Take the first step by scheduling an appointment with a wealth advisor to establish a custom financial plan that will get you closer to your goals. Believe me, you'll be glad you did.

Best of luck to you and planning *your* retirement!

—Jake Falcon, CRPC®

Acknowledgments

To my wonderful wife Rachel, who supports, encourages, and loves me. Without her, I wouldn't be the advisor and man I am today.

To my family for challenging me to be the best version of myself.

To my team at Falcon Wealth Advisors. Cory Bittner, CRPC® for assisting me with content curation for this book. Matthew Tomlin, CFP®, Joe Ibarra, CPA, and Jake Cross, CFP® for editing and reviewing to make sure we produced meaningful content. And to the rest of our team members who wholeheartedly come in and give it their all every day for our clients.

To Tracy Walker, Mark Chait, and the entire team at Scribe for helping me articulate my thoughts in a format that almost any corporate employee can appreciate.

To my clients, who continue to inspire and challenge me daily. Thank you.

Jake

Disclosures

TAX DISCLAIMER

Hightower Advisors, LLC is an SEC registered investment adviser. Securities are offered through Hightower Securities, LLC member FINRA and SIPC. Hightower Advisors, LLC or any of its affiliates do not provide tax or legal advice. This material is not intended or written to provide and should not be relied upon or used as a substitute for tax or legal advice. Information contained herein does not consider an individual's or entity's specific circumstances or applicable governing law, which may vary from jurisdiction to jurisdiction and be subject to change. Clients are urged to consult their tax or legal advisor for related questions.

HIGHTOWER MARKET COMMENTARY DISCLAIMER

Falcon Wealth Advisors is a group comprised of investment professionals registered with Hightower Advisors, LLC, an SEC registered investment adviser. Some investment professionals may also be registered with Hightower Securities, LLC, member

FINRA and SIPC. Advisory services are offered through Hightower Advisors, LLC. Securities are offered through Hightower Securities, LLC. This is not an offer to buy or sell securities. No investment process is free of risk, and there is no guarantee that the investment process or the investment opportunities referenced herein will be profitable. Past performance is neither indicative nor a guarantee of future results. The investment opportunities referenced herein may not be suitable for all investors. All data or other information referenced herein is from sources believed to be reliable. Any opinions, news, research, analyses, prices, or other data or information contained in this presentation is provided as general market commentary and does not constitute investment advice. Falcon Wealth Advisors and Hightower Advisors, LLC or any of its affiliates make no representations or warranties express or implied as to the accuracy or completeness of the information or for statements or errors or omissions, or results obtained from the use of this information. Falcon Wealth Advisors and Hightower Advisors, LLC assume no liability for any action made or taken in reliance on or relating in any way to this information. The information is provided as of the date referenced in the document. Such data and other information are subject to change without notice. This document was created for informational purposes only; the opinions expressed herein are solely those of the author(s) and do not represent those of Hightower Advisors, LLC, or any of its affiliates.

THE CALLAN PERIODIC TABLE OF INVESTMENT RETURNS DISCLAIMER

Callan was founded as an employee-owned investment consulting firm in 1973. Ever since, we have empowered institutional clients with creative, customized investment solutions backed by proprietary research, exclusive data, and ongoing education. Today,

Callan advises on more than $3 trillion in total institutional investor assets, which makes it among the largest independently owned investment consulting firms in the U.S. We use a client-focused consulting model to serve pension and defined contribution plan sponsors, endowments, foundations, independent investment advisers, investment managers, and other asset owners. Callan has six offices throughout the U.S. Learn more at callan.com. Corporate Headquarters: San Francisco Regional Consulting Offices: Atlanta, Chicago, Denver, Portland, and Summit, NJ. The Callan Institute (the "Institute") is, and will be, the sole owner and copyright holder of all material prepared or developed by the Institute. No party has the right to reproduce, revise, resell, disseminate externally, disseminate to any affiliate firms, or post on internal websites any part of any material prepared or developed by the Institute, without the Institute's permission. Institute clients only have the right to utilize such material internally in their business. callan.com.

HIGHTOWER DISCLAIMER

This material does not provide individually tailored investment advice. It has been prepared without regard to the individual financial circumstances and objectives of persons or institution who receive it. Hightower Advisors LLC recommends that investors independently evaluate particular investments and strategies, and encourages investors to seek the advice of a Financial Advisor. The appropriateness of a particular investment or strategy will depend on an investor's individual circumstances and objectives. The information provided has been obtained from sources not associated with Hightower and its associates and shall not in any way be liable for claims, and make no expressed or implied representations or warranties as to the accuracy or completeness

of the data and other information, or for statements or errors contained in or omissions from the obtained data and information referenced herein. Such data and information are subject to change without notice. Neither the information provided nor any opinion expressed constitutes a solicitation for the purchase or sale of any security. No investment process is free of risk, and there is no guarantee that the investment process or the investment opportunities referenced herein will be profitable. Past performance is not indicative of current or future performance. Asset allocation and diversification do not guarantee a profit or protect against a loss. This document was created for informational purposes only.

About the Author

FALCON WEALTH ADVISORS

Falcon Wealth Advisors is a Wealth Management Firm focused on helping clients enhance their financial literacy and empowering them with the knowledge and strategies needed to navigate their financial challenges and accomplish their goals. The firm's mission is to have a lasting positive impact on clients' lives.

JAKE FALCON, CRPC®

Jake Falcon is the founder of wealth management firm Falcon Wealth Advisors which is headquartered in Kansas City. Jake and his company specialize in retirement, financial, and tax planning in conjunction with investment management for corporate employees and high net worth individuals. They currently serve clients in over thirty states.

As a wealth advisor, Jake is committed to helping clients pursue their financial goals, navigate the markets through both good and uncertain times, and preserve their legacies. He has a

particular passion for helping clients prepare for one of the most significant financial life events they will ever face—retirement.

With each client's goals in mind, Jake develops sophisticated, yet straightforward, strategies to help each client achieve his or her personal financial objectives. He monitors both the retirement planning and investment landscape to remain up to date on the latest trends and helps optimize appropriate financial solutions for clients. He also oversees Falcon Wealth Advisors' culture and is dedicated to providing clients with exceptional service.

Jake has a bachelor's degree in business administration from the University of Texas at San Antonio. He holds the Chartered Retirement Planning Counselor℠ (CRPC®) designation and has completed the Investment Strategies and Portfolio Management Executive Education Program at the University of Pennsylvania's Wharton School of Business.

In 2016, *Ingram's* magazine featured Jake in their prestigious "40 Under 40" list. He was also listed in the *Forbes'* 2018, 2019, and 2020 lists of America's Top Next-Gen Wealth Advisors. In 2020, Jake secured the #1 ranking in the state of Kansas. They included Jake in *Forbes'* list of Best-In-State Wealth Advisors for Kansas in 2021 and 2022. In addition, Jake was recognized by AdvisorHub's top 100 Advisors to Watch under $1,000,000,000 in 2023.

In his free time, Jake enjoys playing golf, attending sporting events, traveling, and spending time with his wife, Rachel, and their dog, Einstein.